Consumer Joe

Consumer Joe

Harassing Corporate America, One Letter at a Time

Paul Davidson

Broadway Books / New York

PRINTED IN THE UNITED STATES OF AMERICA

BROADWAY BOOKS and its logo, a letter B bisected on the diagonal, are trademarks of Random House, Inc.

Visit our website at www.broadwaybooks.com

Letter credits: American Egg Board, Circle K Convenience Stores, Cold Stone Creamery, The Hertz Corporation, The HSUS, Jamba Juice, Krispy Kreme Doughnut Corporation, SC Johnson—A Family Company, Skechers USA, Southwest Airlines Co., Taco Bell Corp.

First edition published 2003

Book design by Elizabeth Rendfleisch

Library of Congress Cataloging-in-Publication Data

Davidson, Paul, 1930–
  Consumer Joe : harassing corporate America, one letter at a time / Paul Davidson.
    p.   cm.
   1. Customer services—Humor.   2. Commercial correspondence—Humor.   I. Title.
  HF5415.5.D382 2003
  659.2'02'07—dc21
                                                            2003040311

ISBN 0-7679-1502-X

10 9 8 7 6 5 4 3 2 1

INTRODUCTION

Everyone asks questions. Some people ask the simple ones like, "Are you going to clean up your bedroom?" or "When are you going to take out the garbage?" Some ask the metaphysical ones like, "Is there really a God?" or "What do you think happens to you after you die?" And others ask the stupid ones like, "Would you give me a dollar if I ate this jar filled with razor blades?"

Then there were *my questions*. Would swallowing excessive tooth-paste send me to a poison control center? What would happen to my overnight package if it ended up crashing down on an isolated desert island, much like in the Tom Hanks movie *Cast Away*? Why was Ziploc marketing a "yellow and blue makes green" Ziploc baggy that the colorblind individuals of our world would never be able to use?

They were the questions sparked by America's largest corporations, selling their wares to the American public: fast food, items of personal hygiene, health food, clothing, automobiles, air travel, chocolate covered nuts concealed under a sweet candy shell. They were personally involved in every American's life, in one way or another. Yet, when it came to my queries, I had no idea who would be willing or able to answer them. Were there real people behind the polished corporate logos? Would they take my questions seriously? Would I be able to turn the results into a bestselling book that would grant me the financial freedom to never have to work another day in my life? I quickly slapped myself back into reality, grabbed a packet of Top Ramen for dinner, and started writing.

Enter "David Paulson." Like a chameleon changing colors, I went deep undercover. Using my limited knowledge of the witness relocation program, I cleverly took the "son" from my last name and added it to my first. Then, quietly and without incident, I executed the master-stroke of a "switcheroo." The transformation was completely successful. And frankly, quite laughable. But still, if I was going to find out the answers to all the questions that had filled up my head, I was going to make damn sure no one could come after me, find me, and slap me silly.

My goal in it all was to show that no matter the question, no matter the comment, no matter how strange my ideas may have been, America's largest corporations, however gigantic and impersonal they appeared, would embrace my questions with open arms. They would reach out, slather me with gobs of personal attention, and give me the answers I was looking for. And while doing so, I would finally lay to rest the questions that a large portion of this country had been asking themselves behind closed doors and drawn curtains for years. I mean, c'mon—how many of you have wondered quietly in your close circles of friends just why it is that Cap'n Crunch cereal rips up the roof of your mouth? You know you have. And that's why this book is here.

Not every company reacted as cooperatively as the ones contained in this book. Some were afraid. Others were cautious. A select few couldn't quite understand that David Paulson and Paul Davidson were the same person. But the ones who did, did so with personality and dedication. There were real people out there, behind the corporate curtain, excited and enthusiastic in their responses. Whether or not they felt I deserved some rest in a psychiatric facility, they still extended a helping hand. People helping people. It was a beautiful realization that caused my heart to swell with emotion. (Cue dramatic sweeping orchestral music here.) And all the free coupons I scored didn't hurt either.

So sit back. Grab some of that Sleepytime tea. And open your eyes and your soul to the most mind-bending, earth-shattering collection of stunning information you've ever seen. The kind that changes people. The kind that ushers in Peace on Earth. Or, you know, the kind that makes some really damn good bathroom reading.

Enjoy.

Consumer Joe

September 17, 2001

Barnes & Noble Booksellers
10850 W Pico Blvd
Los Angeles, CA 90064
Attn: Manager

Dear Sir or Madam:

I recently made a trip to your store in Los Angeles, in the market for a set of automotive repair books, a book on how to install sinks and garbage disposals in my own kitchen, and a picture book about the famous boy-band, N'Sync.

While perusing your store's <u>three</u> floors, I found myself both out of breath and fatigued, resulting a shortened trip to your location, and a lack of success in purchasing some of the above books I mentioned.

As a relatively healthy individual, it made me wonder how many people have left your store, fatigued, after attempting to find a particular book of interest. It also gave me a wonderful idea and solution for your West Side Pavilion store.

Since you have so many floors at your disposal, why not provide customers with personal shoppers. Their job, of course, would be to greet consumers as they enter the store, find out the books they want to purchase, and run around the store and fetch them for said consumer. You could recruit young teenagers from local high schools to do these jobs, preferably junior-varsity track runners or cross country runners who have the experience in running long distances without getting tired.

In the meantime, while I await your thoughts on this extremely helpful change for Barnes & Noble Booksellers, I wondered if you might be able to let me know if you have the book, "N'Sync: Larger Than Life". As I said, I never had a chance to purchase it, and with their most recent album, <u>Pop</u>, tearing up the charts, I find myself extremely obsessed with finding out as much as I possibly can about this wonderful boy-band.

Bye, bye, bye,

David Paulson

264 South Doheny Drive, #8 Beverly Hills, CA 90211

BARNES&NOBLE
BOOKSELLERS

September 19, 2001

Dear Mr Paulson,

We do in fact have the book you mentioned NSYNC: Larger Than Life in stock. We will hold the book for you at the front desk under your last name, Paulson. I will pass your suggestion about the personal shoppers along to the home office- however, although we do not have personal shoppers, we do try to provide the best possible customer service that we can. So the next time you visit our store, feel free to ask an employee for assistance. If we have the book in stock, we can get it for you from the shelf- especially if you're worn out! If there is a book you're looking for and we don't have it in stock, we can usually order it from our distributors.

Thank you for your kind letter and suggestion. If you have any other questions our phone number is (310) 475-4144.

Sincerly,

Barnes & Noble

October 4, 2001

Mr. Paul Clayton
CEO
Jamba Juice Corporation
1700 17th Street
San Francisco, CA 94103

Dear Mr. Clayton:

For the life of me, I can't quite understand how people are able to swallow that WHEAT GRASS stuff you grind up for them. I know, it's like eating two pounds of vegetables in one simple little shot of green juice, but quite honestly it tastes like you fell on your face in a game of soccer and just happened to have your mouth open.

However, based on the above trend, I got to thinking. If people are more than willing to pay actual hard-earned money to drink a shot of liquid made from the kind of grass they have in their <u>own</u> <u>backyard</u>... they might just pay to drink some of the following new Jamba Juice flavors I have invented in my spare time:

<u>Tuna Melt</u>: High-in-protein white albacore tuna, some of the juice left behind by it, a mayonnaise/sweet cream, and cheese flavoring.

<u>Thanksgiving Dinner</u>: White or dark meat turkey, cranberry sorbet, gravy flavoring, and heated up in a microwave for about one minute.

<u>Fresh Fish!</u>: Any variety of whatever is the freshest fish at the time of ordering.

Sure, some of these may sound gross or strange, but let's analyze the WHEAT GRASS phenomenon. I think upon further exploration, you'll find that Jamba Juice can emerge as <u>not</u> <u>only</u> the best place to get a drink before Breakfast, but a place to pick up your Lunch and/or Dinner!

I'm looking forward to hearing your thoughts on my above ideas. Please note, these are free for your company to use. All I ask for in return is a mention of my name, or a Jamba Juice created in honor of me.

All juiced up,

David Paulson

264 South Doheny Drive, #8 Beverly Hills, CA 90211

October 9, 2001

David Paulson
264 South Doheny Drive #8
Beverly Hills, Ca 90211

Hello David,

Thank you again for taking the time to contact Jamba Juice. We really appreciate the new flavors you have invented in your spare time. Our research and development department went to work right away in the smoothie lab experimenting with your concoctions.

The Tuna Melt smoothie looks promising. We found the key to be white albacore tuna in oil, lots of mayonnaise and some powdered cheese. However, the Thanksgiving smoothie (turkey, cranberry, and gravy) is posing some challenges. Your recommendation to heat it up would require us to install microwave ovens at all locations. We are consulting with our operations and finance departments to see if this could be a feasible option. Lastly, our blenders are having difficulty mulching the entire fish for the "Fresh Fish" smoothie you mentioned. We are purchasing a "Bass-O-Matic" which is specifically designed to blend fish parts into smooth puree. However, we're like a fish out of water with this one and will need some additional testing before we can place it on our menu board.

In all seriousness, I have included some information on wheatgrass that you might find interesting. Whatever you may think about it, we have numerous Customer testimonials that swear wheatgrass has changed their life for the better. You should give it another try.

Sincerely,

Barry Dinsmore
Customer Service Manager
San Francisco, Ca 94103
1-800-545-9972 X 1138
Email me: bdinsmore@jambajuice.com
www.jambajuice.com

JAMBA JUICE COMPANY
1700 17th STREET
SAN FRANCISCO
CA 94103-5136
phone 415.865.1100
fax 415.487.1143
www.jambajuice.com

December 10, 2001

Mr. Barry Dinsmore
Customer Service Manager
Jamba Juice Corporation
1700 17th Street
San Francisco, CA 94103

Dear Mr. Dinsmore:

Your letter dated October 9th, 2001, found me in great spirits, as I had just received the call from NBC that I had been accepted to be a future contender on their show, "Fear Factor".

As you can imagine, there was a lot of excitement in the air, especially around my apartment, where all of us watch the show with bated breathe, always on the edge of our seat wondering just which people are going to hurl when they try to eat a variety of gross items like bull testicles, pig snouts, and plain 'ol animal blood. Then something reminded me of you, and I had to shoot you off a letter.

Don't you find it interesting that "Fear Factor" or "Survivor" have never asked Jamba Juice to take part in one of those "gross eating challenges" by providing the Players the opportunity to drink down a vile of that bile-ish "wheat grass"? I know you mentioned you have tons of "customer testimonials", but when they didn't accompany your letter I just figured you were kidding around.

Either way, I thought I'd bring up the idea of forcing hapless American citizens to drink your companies green sludge to the Producers of "Fear Factor" if that was okay with you. I just didn't want to step on anyone's toes and then get myself in trouble like I usually do.

Just call me the "green machine",

David Paulson

P.S. – I see a group of people sitting around a pile of grass. Then the host, Joe Rogan, will bring out your CEO who will be wearing the Jamba Juice logo T-shirt (which you can send me if you want me to wear it on the show), and he'll hold everyone's throats open as he pours down the wheat grass. Then people will gag and stuff, and viewer's at home will say to their honeys, "Boy, aren't you glad you don't have to do that!?"

---

264 South Doheny Drive, #8 Beverly Hills, CA 90211

January 3, 2002

David Paulson
264 South Doheny Drive, #8
Beverly Hills, Ca 90211

Dear David:
Thanks for the letter. Congratulations on being picked to appear on "Fear Factor". While your idea to have Jamba represented in some form on national TV is enticing, I worry that we may send the wrong message that our products are "gross".

But what the heck…test the waters. I have included a Jamba T-shirt for you to enjoy. Let me know when you will be on the show…I hope you win.

If there is an interest on part of the producers…you know where to reach us.

Sincerely,

Barry Dinsmore
Customer Service Manager
Jamba Juice Company

415-865-1138
415-431-1219 fax

bdinsmore@jambajuice.com

JAMBA JUICE COMPANY
1700 17th STREET
SAN FRANCISCO
CA 94103-5136
p 415.865.1100
f 415.487.1143

October 1, 2001

President & CEO
Coca-Cola Enterprises Inc.
P.O. Box 723040
Atlanta, GA 31139-0040

Dear Sir or Madam:

I'm writing to find out what the Coca Cola Corporation did with all those cans and bottles of "NEW COKE" after the American public refused to drink it?

The reason I ask is due to yet another failing product, ATARI's "E.T. The Extraterrestrial" video game for their Atari 2600 game console. Whether you know it or not, (I'm not sure if Coca Cola was involved in licensing the original movie), that video game did so horribly, and sold so infrequently, that Atari had to literally bury hundreds of thousands of video game cartridges somewhere in a Mid-Western landfill.

Is there a hole somewhere in this country where you dumped all that "NEW COKE"? Or is it packed away somewhere, waiting for a day when the American public will finally get the genius that was "NEW COKE" and chug it all down without a whimper of discontent?

Wouldn't you like to be a pepper too,

David Paulson

264 South Doheny Drive, #8 Beverly Hills, CA 90211

The Coca-Cola Company

COCA-COLA PLAZA
ATLANTA, GEORGIA

ADDRESS REPLY TO
P. O. BOX 1734
ATLANTA, GA 30301
1-800-438-2653

October 15, 2001

Mr. David Paulson
264 S. Doheny Dr., No. 8
Beverly Hills, CA 90211

Dear Mr. Paulson:

Thank you for your letter. We appreciate your interest in our company
and Coke II.

You asked about Coke II, previously called new Coke, and what happened
to the product. After extensive test marketing, we introduced new Coke
in April of 1985. New Coke had a different formula than the original
Coca-Cola. Our research proved consumers had shown a preference for
this new formula. Shortly after the introduction of new Coke, however,
we reintroduced the original formula as Coca-Cola classic. This
original formula quickly regained its number-one position in the
marketplace.

You can be assured that we did not dump all of the new Coke product
into a landfill. You may be interested to know that Coke II is still
available in select markets today.

If you have additional questions, please contact us again.

Sincerely,

Consumer Affairs Specialist

October 26, 2001

Consumer Affairs Specialist
Coca-Cola Enterprises Inc.
P.O. Box 1734
Atlanta, GA 30301

Dear Consumer Affairs Specalist:

You can imagine how relieved I was to hear that the Coca Cola Corporation has not, in fact, dumped all of the surplus Coke II into a mid-western landfill. I was surprised, however, to find out that Coke II (a.k.a. New Coke) is still available in selected markets today.

What determines which markets get their crack at continuing to drink the left-over Coke II? Is it smaller, rural communities that don't have the power to fight back against Coca Cola and demand a better product? Or is it communities that are on record as "having loved" Coke II when it first was released?

I would love to stockpile a bunch of your Coke II but have had no luck in finding it throughout all of Los Angeles. Can you tell me where in Los Angeles I may be able to find this elusive elixir? I'm dying for it!

Just think about how funny it would be to bring a six-pack of Coke II to a party, and have people wonder if I personally had to dig it up from a Midwestern landfill. People will laugh for hours!

Sincerely,

David Paulson

264 South Doheny Drive, #8 Beverly Hills, CA 90211

The Coca-Cola Company

COCA-COLA PLAZA
ATLANTA, GEORGIA

ADDRESS REPLY TO
P. O. BOX 1734
ATLANTA, GA 30301
——
1-800-438-2653

November 7, 2001

Mr. David Paulson
264 S. Doheny Dr., No. 8
Beverly Hills, CA 90211

Dear Mr. Paulson:

Thank you for your letter. We appreciate your interest in Coke II.

Coke II is available in various areas in the U.S. Local bottling companies choose which products to sell in their area, basing their decisions on consumer demand and other market factors.

You may wish to contact the bottler in your area regarding availabilty. You can reach them at 1-877-878-8280.

Please contact us again if you have additional comments or questions.

Sincerely,

Consumer Affairs Specialist

September 1, 2001

Mr. John D. Williams, Jr.
Executive Director
National SCRABBLE® Association
P.O. Box 700
403 Front Street
Greenport, New York 11944

Dear Executive Director Williams, Jr.:

As an avid Scrabble player, and someone extremely interested in words and letters of the English language, I must commend you on your Association's effort in keeping the game of Scrabble on the forefront of every American's mind.

I'm writing you today, because I have come up with, what I believe to be a way to take Scrabble into the next generation. As the game has remained the same in its rules and strategies since its inception, I believe the time has come for Scrabble to become "hip".

My idea concerns the moment in the game when someone decides that a Player has put a word on the board that, they believe, is incorrect. Today, in its present form, that Player will "challenge" them, thus looking in a Dictionary and checking to see if the placed word is indeed, correct. If the word is nowhere to be found in the Dictionary, that Player must remove the letters and give up his or her turn.

In what I have denoted as "Super Scrabble", each Player will be attached to an electric Dictionary, which will in turn be plugged into an electric wall socket. When a Player is challenged, the word placed on the board will be typed into the electronic Dictionary. If that word is incorrect, the Dictionary itself will send a harmless electrical shock to the incorrect Player, shooting electricity through their entire body.

As I said, the shock will do no permanent damage (trust me, I've tested it many times), but will add a sense of excitement and dread to Players trying to cheat with incorrect words. It also adds that "extra something" that will appeal to the younger set, those of the video game generation.

I currently have a mock-up electric Dictionary that I've created that I'd be happy to demonstrate to you, if interested. I don't make it out to New York too often, but I'd be happy to meet you somewhere halfway. Possibly Missouri or Indianapolis.

S,I,N,C,E,R,E,L,Y,

David Paulson

P.S. – If you don't like the above idea, you could start small by starting to include more of the letter "Z", and add a tile for "Qu", which would at least throw some unknowns into the mix.

264 South Doheny Drive, #8 Beverly Hills, CA 90211

September 12, 2001

Mr. David Paulson
264 South Doheny Drive
#8
Beverly Hills, CA 90211

Dear Mr. Paulson:

I tried to call you today to respond to your recent letter but, sadly, the telephone company has no record of you.

Thanks for your fascinating idea for putting more zap into the SCRABBLE game. Unfortunately, the idea has been around for many years. It was first proposed to the game's original manufacturer, Selchow & Righter, in the early 1950's by a WW II veteran who drew on his experiences playing the game at a Japanese prisoner of war camp.

Development of the idea proved problematic. Human injuries during testing raised the red flag among corporate legal departments as far as product liability and the company was unable to come up with a cost-effective way to manufacture the new unit. Worse, tournament experts were unable to agree on the appropriate voltage for a misspelled or illegitimate word.

I hope you are not too disappointed that we are unable to follow up on your suggestion. We always like to hear from the SCRABBLE-loving public and feel the healthy exchange of new ideas is never a trivial pursuit.

K,E,E,P A,T I,T

John D. Williams Jr.
Executive Director
National SCRABBLE Association

JDW;hs
Cc: Ted L. Nancy, Scrabble R&D dept

PO BOX 700   403 FRONT STREET   GREENPORT NY 11944
(631) 477-0033 · info@scrabble-assoc.com   · www.scrabble-assoc.com · FAX (631) 477-0294

September 25, 2001

Mr. John D. Williams, Jr.
Executive Director
National SCRABBLE® Association
P.O. Box 700
403 Front Street
Greenport, New York 11944

Dear Executive Director Williams, Jr.:

Let me first apologize for not being available to take your call. After experiencing a certain run in with the VP of Human Resources at Burger King Corp. (who seemed to think my unwavering requests for a "Burger King Adult Bib" was a bit on the obsessive side), I had my name and number unlisted for reasons I'd prefer not to get into at the present time.

As for your quick response regarding my "Super Scrabble" idea, I must say that I was, in a word, extremely excited and surprised to receive your letter. Although disappointed that the idea had already been introduced in the 50's, harming humans involved in the product testing, I can honestly say I was relieved to know that I can never be held responsible for such injuries as I was too late in suggesting the concept! After all, you and I both know how litigious this country can be.

Based on what you've told me however, and your openness to new ideas, I decided I'd at least dust off one last idea and throw it into the hopper. This idea, is for a product I like to call, "Scrabble Chewing Gum". Simply put, each stick is not a stick, but eight to ten pieces of gum in the shape of Scrabble tiles. But here's the catch: every pack of gum will include _different_ letters. That way, collectors will strive to find the "gum" letters that spell words they'd like to eat! And for kids, who chew gum incessantly, there's a learning element to sounding like "cows chewing cud".

Again, for all I know, this too was introduced in another decade, but I had to at least try. Isn't that what being an American in this country is all about?

S,I,N,C,E,R,E,L,Y,

David Paulson

P.S. – As Executive Director, I'd be surprised if you didn't have signed headshots/pictures available for your "fans" – me, being one of them. Any chance you could send me one for my game closet?

---

264 South Doheny Drive, #8 Beverly Hills, CA 90211

September 28, 2001

Mr. Michael P. Mack
President and CEO
Garden Fresh Restaurant Corp.
17180 Bernardo Center Dr.
San Diego, CA 92128-2002

Dear Mr. Mack:

As an avid fan of your SOUP PLANTATION restaurants, I must commend you on giving people the opportunity to eat well beyond their means for the low, low price of $7.99.

However, I have been quite concerned lately upon visiting your Los Angeles restaurant – it appears as if a large number of patrons eat to the point of not being able to get up and leave your establishment once they're finished. While, at first, it's quite a comical scene to watch individuals who have stretched their inner-stomach lining to capacity, try to navigate their way through your turnstile exits – deep down, it disturbs me.

Mr. Mack, the reality of this country is this... People will eat anything you put in front of them. Give them a plate stacked with food, ten feet high, and they will proceed to eat all ten feet worth. But, give them a well-portioned meal, and they may have dessert after, but won't have to chug a bottle of Peptol Bismol when they get home.

My idea is this. Don't let your patrons eat "as much as they want"! Give them a menu. A set list of meals to choose from. Then, once they've chosen what they're going to eat, that's all they get!! I think it'll solve the problem of injuries in your exit turnstiles, not to mention...it just may turn the United States from one of the most obese countries, into a healthier country. And you, Mr. Mack, could take one-hundred percent of the credit for your wonderful new (health-conscious) idea!

What do you think?

Healthy and always just-about satisfied,

David Paulson

264 South Doheny Drive, #8 Beverly Hills, CA 90211

SOUPLANTATION & SWEET TOMATOES
17180 BERNARDO CENTER DRIVE
SAN DIEGO, CALIFORNIA 92128

PHONE 858/675-1600

FAX 858/675-1616

October 5, 2001

David Paulson
264 South Doheny Drive #8
Beverly Hills, CA 90211

Dear David:

On behalf of Michael Mack, President and CEO, thank you for taking the time to write and share your praise and suggestions for our restaurants. We appreciate hearing from our guests. As you well know, Souplantation is a unique concept. We provide fresh, wholesome food in a relaxing and friendly environment. While your observations about a few guests overindulging are certainly accurate, at this time we are not considering changing the concept to a menu, portioning and table service. Our restaurants provide our guests with a wide range of variety and tastes. It's the freedom to choose that is appealing to most of our guests, and we are happy to provide it. I know that people are being encouraged to be more health conscious and mindful of what they eat. That is the very reason we ensure that we are always serving the freshest and most wholesome food available.

Thank you again for writing. We appreciate your continued patronage of our restaurants. Please accept the enclosed complimentary meal passes as a "thank you" for being our guest. Do let us know if we can serve you in the future.

Sincerely,

Jill Trecker

Jill Trecker
Guest Services Manager

Cc: Michael Mack

GARDEN FRESH RESTAURANT CORP.

December 10, 2001

Ms. Jill Trecker
Guest Services Manager
Garden Fresh Restaurant Corp.
17180 Bernardo Center Dr.
San Diego, CA 92128-2002

Dear Ms. Trecker:

First and foremost, I wanted to thank you for the generous "Complimentary Meal" coupons that you sent me back on October 5, 2001. Needless to say, it was a welcomed surprise from one of my favorite buffet-style restaurants.

I will say, however, that I find it alarming that you don't seem concerned one bit that "a few guests overindulging is certainly accurate" but that you're "not considering changing the concept to a menu, portioning and table service."

On a recent visit to your Los Angeles location, I met a man named Ralph Evans. Mr. Evans and I met near the front of your store, at your EXIT TURNSTILE. Mr. Evans, unfortunately was extremely overweight, and <u>stuck</u> in your turnstile. I shoved at him with all my might, eventually squeezing him through and allowing him his freedom. Before leaving, I suggested to Mr. Evans that your company may someday consider portioning out your meals, to which Mr. Evans shed a tear. He looked at me, and quite honestly cried out the phrase, "If only <u>someone</u> would do something to help me. God help me. I can't do anything to stop my own gluttony".

It was a heart-wrenching moment, and it motivated me to <u>once again</u> draft a letter to you and try to appeal to the skinny person inside of you. The skinny person who doesn't have an eating disorder. Who doesn't have to worry about exercise. People like Mr. Evans are hurting inside, and quite honestly, if it wasn't for your establishment and the never-ending selection of pizza, clam chowder, and the make-your-own-sundae bar, Mr. Evans might have never needed my help that dark afternoon.

All I ask is that you think about what I'm saying, and let me know what you and Mr. Mack plan on doing about this.

Kindest regards,

David Paulson

P.S. – I know I may sound over-emotional about this issue, but you must understand that I once had a hamster as a child (who's name was Sleepy because hamsters happen to be nocturnal animals and sleep all day, although does a five-year old child happen to know that when he's naming a hamster...I think not)...and Sleepy was overweight. And that's what killed him. Just so you know.

---

264 South Doheny Drive, #8 Beverly Hills, CA 90211

October 3, 2001

Mr. Doug Ducey
CEO & President
Cold Stone Creamery Headquarters
16101 N. 82nd Street, #A4
Scottsdale, AZ 85260

Dear Mr. Ducey:

Although quite a big fan of your COLD STONE CREAMERY ice-cream parlors, I am a little concerned about how sanitary it really is -- mushing up people's ice cream and toppings together on a block of marble for all the world to see.

Let me put it to you this way... I tried mixing ice cream and crushed Oreo's on a piece of marble I purchased just for an experiment. I made the ice cream, walked away, and came back two hours later to try it again. And what do you know, the marble was already smelly and seemed ready to accept mold and germs.

In your stores, your personnel crunch up peoples ice cream and toppings on <u>the</u> <u>same</u> piece of stone, over and over and over again. All day long. Aren't you the least bit concerned that this a tad unsanitary and dangerous?

Sincerely,

David Paulson

P.S. – I read somewhere that your favorite ice cream is "sweet cream" with "black cherries and graham cracker pie crust"! Believe it or not, that's my favorite, too!! But it hasn't always been. When I was growing up in rural Alabama, I found that coconut ice cream with almonds seemed to make the summer months go by much quicker than the typical sweet cream variety.

---

264 South Doheny Drive, #8 Beverly HIlls, CA 90211

October 11, 2001

Mr. David Paulson
264 S. Doheny Dr., #8
Beverly Hills, CA 90211

Dear Mr. Paulson:

Thank you for your interest in Cold Stone Creamery. We are always glad to hear from people like you who are fans of our ice cream, and appreciate having the ability to respond to your questions or concerns.

I thought your attempt to replicate what we do in our stores was quite ingenious. However, our equipment and operational procedures are designed with the latest food safety procedures in mind, which often cannot be duplicated in a home kitchen.

For example, our stones are solid, polished granite, which is harder and less porous than marble. Additionally, our stones are kept at a temperature of approximately 15°F when they are in use, which is too low of a temperature for bacteria to grow. We also train our crew members to scrape the stone between mixing ice cream creations, thereby reducing the possibility of cross-contamination. Finally, as a final safety measure, we clean and sanitize our stones each evening.

Again, we appreciate hearing from you and hope that we've adequately addressed your concerns. If you have any additional questions please feel free to contact me directly at (480) 348–1704 ext 104.

Sincerely,

Cold Stone Creamery

October 4, 2001

El Torito Restaurants, Inc.
4001 Via Oro Avenue, Suite 200
Long Beach CA 90810
Attn: Customer Relations

Dear Sir or Madam:

Enclosed please find $1.00 (one dollar), for your "Give Us A Dollar and We'll Give You A Weeks Worth of Meals On Us!!" Promotion.

As the rules specifically state, you will also find my Haiku poem below, which will explain why I should be awarded a "week's worth of free dinners" at any of your West Coast establishments.

I love to eat beans,
It makes my day so happy,
Munch, munch, crunch – oh yeah!

In addition, per your request, the twelve words that best describe my personality while eating at any of your establishments are: *happy, confident, hungry, social, pleased, joyous, drunk* (sometimes), *funny, likeable, loving, gracious,* and *one-hundred percent satisfied* (even though that's three or four words!).

Thank you for sponsoring such a wonderfully challenging contest!

Soy muy loco,

David Paulson

Enclosure:
$1 Dollar Bill

---

264 South Doheny Drive, #8 Beverly Hills, CA 90211

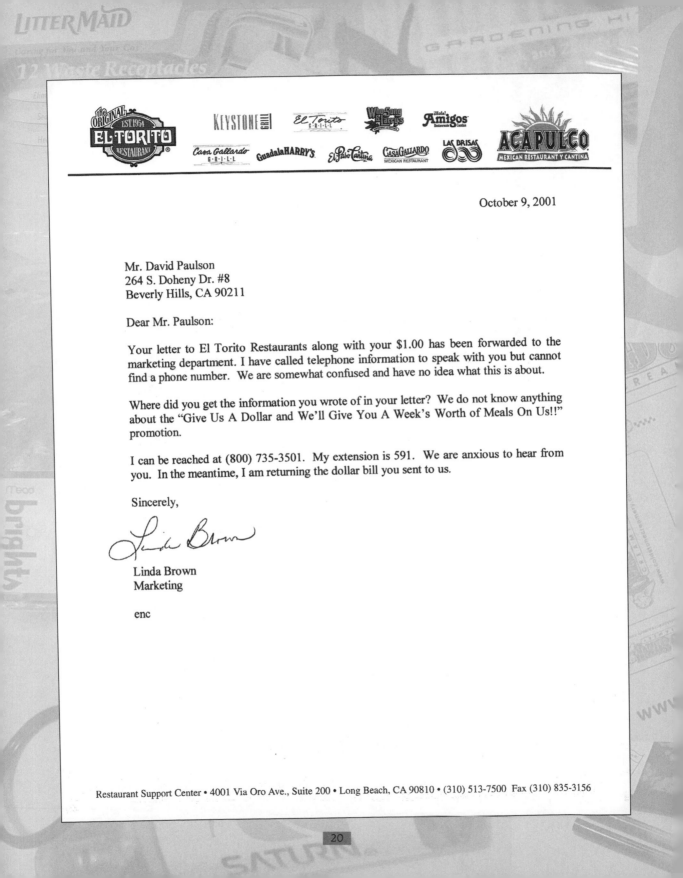

October 9, 2001

Mr. David Paulson
264 S. Doheny Dr. #8
Beverly Hills, CA 90211

Dear Mr. Paulson:

Your letter to El Torito Restaurants along with your $1.00 has been forwarded to the marketing department. I have called telephone information to speak with you but cannot find a phone number. We are somewhat confused and have no idea what this is about.

Where did you get the information you wrote of in your letter? We do not know anything about the "Give Us A Dollar and We'll Give You A Week's Worth of Meals On Us!!" promotion.

I can be reached at (800) 735-3501. My extension is 591. We are anxious to hear from you. In the meantime, I am returning the dollar bill you sent to us.

Sincerely,

Linda Brown
Marketing

enc

Restaurant Support Center • 4001 Via Oro Ave., Suite 200 • Long Beach, CA 90810 • (310) 513-7500 Fax (310) 835-3156

October 18, 2001

Ms. Linda Brown
El Torito Restaurants, Inc.
4001 Via Oro Avenue, Suite 200
Long Beach CA 90810

Dear Ms. Brown:

You can imagine that I was quite excited when the local postman delivered a slip into my mailbox from your company – and CERTIFIED, at that! I had won your contest, with my clever Haiku, was the first thought that entered my head. Unfortunately, my quick trip to the post office, which caused me to get a ticket for rolling through a stop sign, was not as joyous as I had originally thought.

My main concern, Ms. Brown, is that I am going to be way past the deadline for your promotion based on the fact that I don't have a phone number listed. If you must know, I've had a lot of trouble with the Myers kids (Kyle and Ralphie), who spend most of their spare time after 3pm (that's when school gets out) harassing and haranguing me. Between writing slanderous words on my garbage cans ("STUPID CHEESE HEAD") and putting empty plastic bottles underneath my rear tires, they also like to crank call me. Thus the unlisted number. I'm happy to say, it at least provided me some well-needed peace and quiet.

As for where I heard about your ingenious contest promotion, it was posted on a flyer at the Kinko's on Wilshire Boulevard here in Beverly Hills – just down the street from your El Torito Grill. But it's obvious to me that alone, a flyer could be misleading, but I had also heard of the promotion via Becky Ainsely, a woman I know from kickboxing class.

I don't know if you realized after creating the promotion that it would cost your corporation too much money to pay off the winners, or that you felt my Haiku was too good that it would ruin the competition for the rest of the entries. Either way, I think I deserve to know the answer, as you've returned my dollar, and I've only got until November 30th to get this thing going!! And since I've already lost the POP SECRET and PILLSBURY contests, this one is my last chance.

KIndest regards,

David Paulson

P.S. – I have not returned the dollar and will not return the dollar until you have responded and let me know what my next step should be.

Enclosure:
Nothing Whatsoever

---

264 South Doheny Drive, #8 Beverly Hills, CA 90211

September 1, 2001

Saturn Corporation
100 Saturn Parkway
Mail drop S-24
Spring Hill, TN 37174
Attn: Customer Service Dept.

Dear Sir or Madam:

Let me first say that I'm a satisfied Saturn customer, having had my Saturn SL1 since 1995, and except for two minor accidents, replacing the brake-pads, an alternator problem, and some minor recall having to do with the driver's side seat bolts, it's been pretty smooth sailing.

The reason I'm writing, however, is in regards to your logo. I find it awfully strange that you named your car company after a planet that no one has ever been to. What happens if one day it's uncovered that Saturn is simply a planet made up of dangerous and toxic gases? You don't want your car company associated with that garbage.

Based on N.A.S.A.'s current schedule (available at www.nasa.gov), they will be sending un-manned probes to Saturn in 2012, 2015, and 2017 and it strikes me that you're playing with fire unless you do something to involve yourself in these future missions. At least, that way, you can hush up any negative discoveries (much like N.A.S.A. has done with the Face on Mars), and keep your company's image in a positive light.

Otherwise, you may want to think about changing your name to something that guarantees positive connotations. Pick the Moon, for example. It's solid, unwavering, and always there for you. Or what about The Milky Way Galaxy itself? It's mysterious, but dazzling, an eye-catcher, and all-encompassing. Maybe Moon Cars, or Milky Way Galaxy Cars would be something to put into the machine, you know, see how people feel about that?

From your Saturn SL1 owner,

David Paulson

P.S. – Any chance you could send me a free key-chain or something with your logo on it? These things are going to be worth something, someday, when you change your name!

264 South Doheny Drive, #8 Beverly Hills, CA 90211

MR. DAVID PAULSON
264 SOUTH DOHENY DRIVE
BEVERLY HILLS, CA 90211

Hello David,

Thank you for your letter concerning the future of the Saturn logo. Your comments have been documented and forwarded to the appropriate management team for review. Please enjoy the key chain and we hope it brings you much use and happiness.

Sincerely,
Michael Lovell
Saturn Customer
Assistance Center.

December 11, 2001

Mr. Michael Lovell
Saturn Customer Assistance Center
Saturn Corporation
P.O. Box 300
Spring Hill, TN 37174-0300

Dear Mr. Lovell:

I'm getting a tad worried. Everywhere I look I see Saturn cars. There are commercials, fliers, radio advertisements. And all with the same logo and name that you had the last time I wrote you a letter on September 1st.

I don't know if you thought I was just joking, but NASA will find out sooner than later that the planet of Saturn is made up of poisonous gases. Then what will you all do? Start up a new radio campaign that informs Saturn owners that your cars "are explosively exciting?" That they pick up speed like "a fireball"? I think not.

Would you be so kind as to let me know who, <u>exactly</u>, you forwarded my previous letter to? You said it went to "the appropriate management team for review". Who are they? Where can I reach them? What are their names and titles?

On a completely different note – thanks for the key-chain. When can I expect the T-shirt that you promised?

From your Saturn SL1 owner,

David Paulson

P.S. – I'm a LARGE, in cotton T's.

---

264 South Doheny Drive, #8 Beverly Hills, CA 90211

September 28, 2001

Saturn Corporation
100 Saturn Parkway
Mail drop S-24
Spring Hill, TN 37174
Attn: Customer Service Dept.

Dear Sir or Madam:

On a recent trip to your Saturn Airport Marina location, I spotted a car that I thought would be a great addition to my garage.

Unfortunately, upon speaking with one of your car salesmen, it was brought to my attention that he would allow no "haggling or negotiating" whatsoever. "The price on the car is the price that we sell it for", he stated.

Are you kidding me? How long is it that your company has been pulling this one off on the consumers of America? And how many people have "fallen" for this gigantic ruse?

Kindest regards,

David Paulson

Saturn Corporation
Customer Assistance Center
100 Saturn Parkway
P.O. Box 1500
Spring Hill, TN 37174-1500
Telephone (800) 553-6000

October 19, 2001

David Paulson
264 S. Doheny Dr., #8
Beverly Hills, CA   90211

Dear David:

Thank you for taking the time to contact Saturn Corporation regarding your pricing concern.

We encourage our retailers to make the shopping and buying experience pleasurable. For this reason, our no-hassle, no-haggle pricing has become an integral part of Saturn's buying experience. Saturn Corporation does not "fix prices." We simply provide a Manufacturer's Suggested Retail Price (MSRP), and each retailer sets pricing for the product sales and service. However, once the retailers have set their prices, we ask them to adhere to those prices for every customer. That way, no customer has to worry, "Is the next guy getting a better deal?"

We strongly believe our vehicles are competitive at the MSRP levels, and they offer outstanding quality and substantially exceed the competition in overall value. We also believe a Saturn retail facility must earn sufficient profit to allow it to have the necessary facilities, tools, and personnel to service customers adequately before, during, and after the sale of the car.

If you ever have any questions or concerns, please feel free to contact the Saturn Customer Assistance Center at 1-800-553-6000, prompt 3. One of our customer care consultants will be happy to assist you.

Once again, thank you for considering Saturn in your search for an automobile. Please let us know if there is any additional information we can provide.

Sincerely,

James A. Moses

James A. Moses
Saturn Customer Assistance Center

A Subsidiary of General Motors

 recycled paper

September 6, 2001

Applica
Service & Repair Department
5980 Miami Lakes Drive
Miami Lakes, FL 33014

Dear Sir or Madam:

I recently purchased your Littermaid Self Cleaning Litterbox for my cats Scrunches, Vittles, and David Paymer - named after the guy who played the bus driver in <u>Hearts & Souls</u>. You may or may not remember that movie, but it starred Robert Downey, Jr. as a grown-up who could talk to his guardian angels. Really, it wasn't his best work, but it was before all his drug problems, so you have to like it at least for that.

In any case, I must tell you that your Self Cleaning Litterbox has caused my cat David Paymer a lot of pain, not to mention costing me an arm and a leg at the Vet. On July 24th, as I was watching TV, I heard a grinding sound from the kitchen (where I keep the litterbox). I jumped up when I heard David Paymer screeching, and ran in to find his left hind-leg caught in the mechanism. As it was trying to clean the box, it has grabbed David Paymer and cracked his bone.

Needless to say, I was not happy with the outcome. For some reason, my Littermaid Litterbox does not wait until the cats have done their business, and left the box. Instead, it lashes out and tries to get them. I don't know if this is a malfunctioning computer mechanism or what, but David Paymer won't go near it again. I've had to resort to putting two litterboxes side by side in my kitchen, which makes it smell horrendous.

I'm hoping that your customer service department will see fit to do something to rectify the situation. Maybe you have a t-shirt or something you could send me? Or something for David Paymer to play with? Some cat-nip?

Meow...Crunch,

David Paulson

264 South Doheny Drive, #8 Beverly Hills, CA 90211

December 11, 2001

Applica
Service & Repair Department
5980 Miami Lakes Drive
Miami Lakes, FL 33014

Dear Sir or Madam:

 This is David Paymer. As of three-weeks ago, he has been missing. This is due to your company's faulty Littermaid Self Cleaning Litterbox.

David Paymer (named after the character actor from such movies as Hearts & Souls and The Larry Sanders Show), got his left paw caught in the grinding jaws of my Littermaid Litterbox months ago – which resulted in a letter I sent to the above address.

Your staff, in what must have seemed like a hilarious joke, sent me two additional packets of waste receptacles for the same litter box that injured Mr. Paymer. You can imagine the fear that crossed David's face when he saw the UPS man deliver them on that dark day. But we pressed on. Using my best friend's animal psychologist, who simply goes by the name of "The Mystical One", we tried our best to re-introduce the wonderful little David Paymer to his "friendly" Self Cleaning Litterbox.

Three weeks ago he relapsed. Having yet another run-in with the plastic jaws of your behemoth sand cruncher, Mr. Paymer jumped out the kitchen window and has been missing ever since. I hold Applica personally responsible for this matter and am writing to find out just what you're going to do about the missing and talented David Paymer.

Had David Paymer returned home to me, like the little talented bastard should have, I would not have written this letter. But now, as the future appears dark, the last option was this. I'm sure you understand.

I look forward to your timely response in this matter.

Sadly,

David Paulson

264 South Doheny Drive, #8 Beverly Hills, CA 90211

September 24, 2001

Mr. Mark T. Watkins
Vice President, Technology
The Mead Corporation
World Headquarters
Courthouse Plaza Northeast
Dayton, OH 45463

Dear Mr. Watkins:

First of all, I have to apologize for missing the opportunity to congratulate you on your promotion to Vice President of Technology back in November 2000. Syracuse "Orangemen" really need to stick together, and well, I quite honestly dropped the ball!

But you know how people always say that timing really is important? For example, if I hadn't been in the market for a miniature Chihuahua at the same time that Tanaka was born, well, I wouldn't have ended up with the perfect little housemate! Same goes for me writing to you – if I had written you this letter when you were working in Human Resources, well, you would really have had no power to put these ideas in motion.

Here's the thing. I've been thinking about your company's Trapper Keeper products for kids. These things are wonderful, and they're always packed with the greatest little gadgets. Pencil and pen holders, Velcro latches, extra-sturdy construction for those drops on the playground...you guys have really kept things going in the "advances" area. But there's one thing you're missing. A compass.

Think about how many times we hear about "lost children". If only they had a compass built into their Trapper Keepers! Then, as long as their parents had instructed them on how to use it, I think you'd see the missing children numbers really decline. Not to mention, how many times do kids want to go camping <u>and</u> work on their homework. Tons of times, if my neighborhood is any example. But more often than not, homework takes a back seat to camping gear.

Not any more. It's quite possible that if your company creates a partnership with a camping company such as REI, you may have a hit on your hands. In the meantime, I'm going to go ahead and cc: the President of REI (Dennis Madsen) on this letter so the two of you can get things moving.

Again, congratulations on the promotion, and I hope this little piece of "insider information" is helpful to you. If you're pleased by my dedication, maybe you can send me my own Trapper Keeper or pack of pencils!!

Go Orangemen!

David Paulson

DP/hdm
cc: Dennis Madsen, REI International

---

264 South Doheny Drive, #8 Beverly Hills, CA 90211

The Mead Corporation
Courthouse Plaza Northeast
Dayton, OH 45463

www.meadweb.com

TEL: 937 495 3189
FAX: 937 495 1712
EMAIL: waw2@mead.com

mead

William A. Wendell
Executive Vice President
Sales & Marketing
Consumer Products Group
Consumer & Office Products

November 2, 2001

Mr. David Paulson
264 South Doheny Drive, #8
Beverly Hills, CA 90211

Dear Mr. Paulson:

Your letter of September 24, to Mr. Mark Watkins was forwarded to me for review and reply.

We are always pleased to get input from the outside regarding our products and any suggestions which may enhance our product offering. Your suggestions for including a compass with our Trapper Keeper® is an interesting one. We must decline your suggestion to partner with a camping company, but do thank you for thinking of Mead and providing your "insider information".

Since our Trapper Keeper® has been around for many years, the line offering has lessened to allow for new and more innovative products. When you're out shopping sometime, you must take a look at our new Smartbook® which comes with either a spell check/calculator, radio, voice memo recorder or multilingual translator. Our complete range of products is listed on the internet at www.meadweb.com.

As you requested, I have enclosed a Trapper XL®. Since we do not manufacture pencils, I have enclosed a pencil pouch.

Again, thank you for your interest in Mead.

Regards,

WAWendell

William A. Wendell

WAW:srg

Enclosures (2)

cc: Mark Watkins
     Neil McLachlan

December 11, 2001

Mr. William A. Wendell
Executive Vice President, Sales & Marketing
The Mead Corporation
World Headquarters
Courthouse Plaza Northeast
Dayton, OH 45463

Dear Mr. Wendell:

Thank you so much for your kind words, dated November 2nd, 2001. It's always a pleasure to get a letter from a bigwig like yourself. I mean, you must look in the mirror each day and smile, thinking to yourself, "I'm the Executive Vice President of Sales and Marketing. Powerful enough to crush all who came before me as well as those who teased me in Junior High." At least, if I was you, that's what I'd be saying.

You can imagine my surprise to find that your company is currently selling the Smartbook® product across the country – and that they include such amazing things as a voice memo recorder and/or multilingual translators. Talk about melding the stories of science-fiction with normal, everyday binders! No wonder you got to where you are today!

So, here I sit now, disappointed that you sent me a normal Trapper XL® instead of what I would have asked for (the Smartbook®), if I had been informed that conventional science had created such a hybrid information booklet/translator. Do you think there's any way for me to exchange what you gave me before, for what I want now? I'd even be happy to send you back the pencil pouch, although I've grown quite fond of it.

Please make sure to say hello to Mark Watkins, and tell him that his fellow Orangeman said "Hey". (We went to the same college, if you must know!)

Give my best to your wife, your family, and "srg", whoever that is.

Most sincere regards,

David Paulson

---

264 South Doheny Drive, #8 Beverly Hills, CA 90211

November 1, 2001

Anheuser-Busch Companies, Inc.
One Busch Place
St. Louis, MO 63118
Attn: Customer Service Department

Dear Sir or Madam:

I weigh one-hundred and ninety pounds and wondered how many Budweisers I would need to drink in order to get buzzed, but not be in danger of getting arrested for public drunkenness.

Kindest Regards,

David Paulson

Anheuser-Busch, Inc.
ONE OF THE ANHEUSER-BUSCH COMPANIES

December 7, 2001

David Paulson
#8
264 S Doheny Dr.
Beverly Hills, CA 90211

Dear Mr. Paulson,

Thank you for writing Anheuser-Busch and asking about the effects of beer consumption on individuals.

We avoid trying to estimate how many beers it will take to affect someone in a particular way, because there are many personal factors involved, among which are a person's sex, body weight, stress levels, and food consumption. All these have an effect on one's blood alcohol content (BAC). Further, state laws and local ordinances differ on the BAC that is deemed appropriate for those on public property or behind the wheel.

Only the person drinking knows how he feels and responds to alcohol on a given day, and that is one of the reasons why we promote personal responsibility - for some, this means no drinking at all. We urge you to consume our products responsibly and in moderation. This includes, for example, choosing a designated driver or using alternate transportation if your evening away from home includes alcohol beverages. This is the best way to avoid problems and respect yourself and the law.

We hope this helps, and we appreciate your letter.

Sincerely,

Jeff Esserman
Manager, Customer Call Center
1-800-DIAL-BUD

jde/cl

2618910B

October 2, 2001

Mr. Emil Brolich
Taco Bell Corporation
17901 Von Karman
Irvine, CA 92614-6221

Dear Mr. Brolich:

Your beans have changed my life, Mr. Brolich!! Whereas I used to spend hours upon hours creating elaborate concoctions in the privacy of my own kitchen, I found it took up so much time I rarely found that I was "really living" my life. Then came your beloved restaurant, Taco Bell, and my life was transformed!!

Only just recently, did the reality of how your corporation works, come to light. I was visiting my local Taco Bell, and realized that your most recent promotion, "Get A Toy With Every Purchase of a Kid's Meal" was somewhat disconcerting. As I'm a kid at heart, I attempted to purchase said Kid's Meal in an attempt to acquire on of your wonderful toys. But I was met with confusion, as I was visiting alone, and "had no children with me". Your staff refused to let me purchase a Kid's Meal because I had no kids with me.

I immediately tried to bribe a few youngsters who were walking into the store at that particular moment, but they were also there to acquire their own toys, and refused me in my advances.

I can't help but wonder, Mr. Brolich, why Taco Bell seeks to alienate its adult consumers? The least your company can do is to create an Adult's Meal that include toys as well. Otherwise, I've either got to get married and adopt a child to get at those collectibles, or live out the rest of my life with a part of me, simply missing. Which one do you think I must endure?

Yo Quiero Toys,

David Paulson

264 South Doheny Drive, #8 Beverly Hills, CA 90211

Taco Bell Corp.
17901 Von Karman
Irvine, CA 92614
Telephone: 949 863 4312
Fax: 949 863 2246

January 4, 2002

Mr. David Paulson
264 S. Doheny Drive #8
Beverly Hills CA 90211

Dear Mr. Paulson:

Thank you for your letter, which was forwarded to the office of the
President of Taco Bell. He has asked me to respond.

First of all, thank you for taking the time to make us aware of your concerns
regarding your visit to one of our Los Angeles area restaurants. I have forwarded
a copy of your letter to the Regional Manager of this area for his review.

We can certainly appreciate your concern and apologize for any inconvenience.
In the meantime, as a token of our appreciation for your comments, I have
enclosed several coupons and hope you will enjoy your next Taco Bell meal with
our compliments.

Sincerely,

Taco Bell

November 5, 2001

National Park Service
P.O. Box 168
Yellowstone National Park, WY 82190

Dear Sir or Madam:

As I'm currently finishing my thesis at UCLA here in Southern California, it was necessary for me to confirm one last piece of information before I put the one-hundred and twelve page project to the printers.

As you may or may not know, Yogi Bear and his little buddy Boo-Boo spent a lot of time in Jellystone Park, causing havoc and annoying Ranger Smith to the point of exhaustion and frustration. Of course, this was all out of a great sense of fun and mischief, but Ranger Smith simply didn't get the memo on that one, and took things way too seriously.

My thesis, called "Exhaustion on the Job: Ranger Smith's National Park Bear Problem", centers primarily on how rangers plagued with mischievous animals can often find themselves tired and fatigued, therefore causing them to make serious mistakes while working on the job at a National Park.

My question is this: Is there any similarity to the "JELLYSTONE PARK" in the Yogi Bear cartoons and "YELLOWSTONE PARK". In addition, has Yellowstone Park ever employed a Ranger with the last name "Smith"?

Sincerely,

David Paulson

264 South Doheny Drive, #8 Beverly Hills, CA 90211

United States Department of the Interior

NATIONAL PARK SERVICE
PO Box 168
Yellowstone National Park
Wyoming 82190

IN REPLY REFER TO:

N1427(YELL)

January 8, 2002

Mr. David Paulson
264 South Doheny Drive, #8
Beverly Hills, California 90211

Dear Mr. Paulson:

We have received your letter requesting comparisons between Yellowstone National Park and the fictional "Jellystone Park." Please accept our apology for the delay in replying.

There is little similarity between present day Yellowstone and the "Jellystone Park" portrayed in the Yogi Bear cartoons. However, historically bears were once commonly observed along roadsides and within developed areas of Yellowstone National Park. Bears were attracted to these areas by the availability of human foods in the form of handouts and unsecured camp groceries and garbage. Although having bears readily visible along roadsides and within developed areas was very popular with the park visitors, it was also considered to be the primary cause of an average of forty-eight bear-caused human injuries per year from 1930 through 1969.

In 1970, Yellowstone initiated an intensive bear management program with the objectives of restoring the grizzly bear and black bear populations to subsistence on natural forage and reducing bear-caused injuries to humans. As part of the bear management program implemented in 1970, regulations prohibiting the feeding of bears were strictly enforced, as were regulations requiring that human food be kept secured from bears. In addition, garbage cans were bear-proofed and garbage dumps within the park were closed. During this period, any bear that developed habits similar to Yogi's, was translocated within or removed from the park, especially if they persisted as a threat to humans.

Although bears are less frequently observed along roadsides and within developed areas today than in the past, many people still see bears each year. If you have any further questions please feel free to contact the Bear Management Office in Yellowstone at (307) 344-2162.

Yellowstone hires many seasonal law enforcement rangers each year, and it is most likely that we've had a "Ranger Smith" on our staff several times over the years. Currently, there are two employees with the surname Smith employed in the park. One is an interpretive ranger, and the other is a supervisory criminal investigator.

Sincerely,

Rick Obernesser
Chief Ranger

September 7, 2001

Top Flight, Inc.
1300 Central Avenue
Chattanooga, TN 37408
Attn: Customer Service

Dear Sir or Madam:

I recently purchased a package of 50 plain white envelopes so that I could send a variety of my friends and relatives the pictures from my most recent birthday party. It was a theme party, if you must know, where everyone had to dress up as their favorite 80's celebrity. I, dressed up as "Crockett" from TV's <u>Miami Vice</u>. But I didn't win the grand prize of Grand Poobah Celebrity – that went to my cousin Fanny, who dressed up as Brigitte Neilsen, the tall blonde Amazon woman from <u>Beverly Hills Cop 2</u>.

In any case, I'm sure you can imagine my displeasure when I opened up the package and counted the envelopes and there were only **forty-seven** of them inside. I immediately went back to my local Rite Aid store where I purchased two more packages. Each, unopened, contained **forty-nine**, and **forty-eight**.

I don't know what you people are trying to pull here by shorting people like me out of letter-sized envelopes, but I can tell you that I don't appreciate it. I buy a box of 50 envelopes because I need 50 envelopes. If I only needed forty-eight envelopes, I'd go to your competitor and buy their box of 48 envelopes.

If you add up the difference here, I was cheated out of six envelopes. At what I paid for this package of envelopes ($1.99), I have calculated that your company owes me a grand total of $0.2388 dollars. It may sound like nothing, but if I bought one-hundred boxes of your envelopes over my lifetime, you'd be getting an extra $23 dollars from me. And that, my Top Flight friends, is unfair. What do YOU think?

Sealed in your product,

David Paulson

P.S. – I would be happy to exchange the $0.2388 for a credit towards another box of <u>50</u> envelopes if that's how you'd like to handle it.

---

264 South Doheny Drive, #8 Beverly Hills, CA 90211

TOP FLIGHT

September 24, 2001

David Paulson
264 S. Doheny Drive #8
Beverly Hills, CA 90211

Dear Mr. Paulson:

Thank you for writing Top Flight.

In your letter you stated you had purchased one of our products at Rite Aid. Rite Aid is not one of our customers. Please send proof-of-purchase and a sample of the problem and if it is our product we will be happy to replace the item.

Thank you for your assistance in this matter.

Sincerely,

TOP FLIGHT, INC.

Bernadette Picou
Customer Service Representative

Cc: M. Robinson
     W. Robinson

1300 Central Avenue
Chattanooga, TN 37408
423-266-8171
FAX 423-266-6857

September 28, 2001

Ms. Bernadette Picou
Top Flight, Inc.
1300 Central Avenue
Chattanooga, TN 37408

Dear Ms. Picou:

You can imagine my chagrin when I received your letter regarding my letter regarding the purchase of your product – and being cheated out of six letter-sized envelopes! The chagrin, of course, was based on the fact that I mentioned I purchased the said referenced products at RITE AID, when in fact, I had purchased them from RALPH'S.

Trust me when I tell you that the last thing I want is pity, but as I am somewhat dyslexic, I often mistake RITE AID with RALPH's. Sure, some people say that dyslexia is when people mix-up and re-arrange letters...but in my case I end up mixing up similar words and names that begin with the same letter. So, if I had purchased your envelopes from TARGET, you can bet money on the fact that I wouldn't have screwed that one up!!

You may think it's hard to confuse RITE AID with RALPH's, simply based on the fact that RALPH's has a great full-service deli and they make cakes for you in-house when you've got that special occasion coming up. But, let's be sure to remember that RITE AID also has food aisles, just not people waiting on you hand and foot to serve you. And you know what? In Europe, people don't get served like they do here in America, so what's the big deal if RITE AID doesn't provide you with a servant every time you enter their store? I say, get over it, develop your film, and buy that package of Twinkees and be on your way.

As per your request for the proof-of-purchases, you can't expect me to have saved empty boxes with nothing in them!! I already used the envelopes and thus, threw out the garbage! (I've been doing my best lately to not hold onto useless items that simply clutter my apartment!) But – as my first letter stated, your company technically owes me the grand total of $0.2388 dollars, for the missing six envelopes that you never provided me.

Personally, I think $0.2388 dollars is a bargain for keeping a customer happy. What do you think, Ms. Picou?

Out of envelopes,

David Paulson

P.S. – I just had to wonder aloud, Ms. Picou, but are you French? If so, can you recommend a good time to visit Paris? My friend Elisha says May or June, but my travel agent says October/November. What do you think?

264 South Doheny Drive, #8 Beverly Hills, CA 90211

October 3, 2001

David Paulson
264 S. Doheny Drive #8
Beverly Hills, CA 90211

Dear Mr. Paulson:

We are very sorry for the shortage you have experienced with the Envelopes you had purchased.

At the beginning of each shift our Supervisors reset every counter on every machine. Even though we are constantly trying to perfect all the mechanical processes involved in making our products, occasionally malfunctions do occur. Apparently this happened with the Envelopes you had purchased. Your letter has been referred to our Production and Quality Control Departments. I assure you they will do everything possible to prevent this from happening again.

We are sending you, under separate cover, one package of item#72119 50 ct. Envelopes. We hope this is an acceptable substitution for you as there is no way for us to know exactly which type of envelope you purchased.

Thank you for writing to us about this problem and we hope you will continue to use our products in the future.

Sincerely,

TOP FLIGHT, INC.

Bernadette Picou
Customer Service Representative

Cc:
    W. Robinson
    M. Robinson

1300 Central Avenue
Chattanooga, TN 37408
423-266-8171
FAX 423-266-6857

September 28, 2001

Hasbro Games
Consumer Affairs Department
P.O. Box 200
Pawtucket, RI 02862

Dear Sir or Madam:

As a child weaned on Ritalin, you can imagine the kind of crazy, out-of-hand mischief I often got myself into. But when my parents put SIMON in front of me, the colorful lights and melodic beeps caused my uncontrollable fits to dissipate, not unlike the mist after a thunder storm. So, on behalf of my parents, thank you for that!

As an adult, you can imagine the frenetic excitement I felt when I came across your new, updated game…SIMON 2. I immediately purchased it, a package of batteries, and raced home to begin playing with my new toy!!

Unfortunately, things turned somewhat dark when I realized that my SIMON 2 had <u>not</u> come with EIGHT RUBBER FEET as it was supposed to, but instead had only come with SEVEN RUBBER FEET. This, of course, put the entire game off balance, and caused irritating scratching and screeching sounds whenever I'd play it on my kitchen counter. And since the kitchen counter is the only place I can play it (as I did when I was a child), I can't play SIMON 2, at all.

I hope you can do me a favor and rush me my EIGHTH RUBBER FOOT as soon as possible. How about FedEx, they can ship things overnight? Or UPS? I don't quite care which way you ship it, as long as it gets here as quickly as possible. Really, I don't want to have to go buy another one just for a RUBBER FOOT. That would be awfully silly, don't you think?

Green, blue, yellow, green,

David Paulson

264 South Doheny Drive, #8 Beverly Hills, CA 90211

October 1, 2001

MR DAVID PAULSON
264 SOUTH DOHENY DR #8
BEVERLY HILLS, CA 90211

Dear MR PAULSON,

Thank you for contacting us regarding our SIMON 2. We appreciate
your bringing this matter to our attention, and apologize for
any inconvenience this may have caused.

If you return the product to us, we will be happy to send a new
replacement product. If there is a production delay and this
product is not available, we will replace it with a product of
equal value. Enclosed is a postage paid label for this
purpose. Our postage paid labels are valid for four weeks from
the date of this letter. Please be advised that we cannot
accept responsibility for uninsured, lost or misdirected mail.
Please include a brief note explaining the problem with the
product, along with your return address and phone number.

We want to assure you that all of us are dedicated to
maintaining quality products. We hope you and your family will
enjoy our products for many years to come.

Please call us at 1-888-836-7025 if we can be of further
assistance.

Sincerely,

CONSUMER AFFAIRS DEPT.

Kerry Bronson
Consumer Affairs Representative
10/01/01 891/1A 2903
KXB/kxb/C0005

enc: Postage Paid label

December 10, 2001

Consumer Affairs Representative
Hasbro, Inc.
200 Narragansett Park Drive
P.O. Box 200
Pawtucket, RI 02862-0200

Dear Sir or Madam:

My Uncle Saul once purchased a brand new BMW 330i from the BMW Dealership here in Beverly Hills. It was a wonderful car, with speed, elegance, and one of those cool trip computers that could tell you at any given time just how many miles you could travel on the gas that was left in the tank. Quite honestly, it was pretty dang awesome.

A few weeks into driving the car around town, which included trips to the local 99 cents store (he had spent his life savings on the car so he wouldn't be caught dead spending 2.99 on a six pack of Snapple), the local Boston Market, and various family events and birthday parties...something happened. Somebody stole <u>one</u> of his hubcaps.

Mind you, this was a brand-new car. One that he had wanted ever since he was a child. He had saved his money, purchased his dream-toy, and one week into his "motor-heaven" someone stole his hubcap. He called his BMW dealer immediately and asked if they'd send him a new one. And do you know what they said? They told him to send back the ENTIRE CAR in a POSTAGE PAID ENVELOPE and they'd send it back to him with the new hubcap. And as I'm sure you're a smart man or woman, you know how silly that sounds.

So, why....Why must I send back my entire SIMON 2 game system simply because your company mistakenly forgot to give me <u>all</u> eight plastic feet, instead only providing me with seven? Why not just send me the ONE PLASTIC FOOT I'm missing and I'll just place it right into my game system?

My Uncle Saul, who just happens to be one of those guys who goes around to companies and tells them if their way of doing things is efficient or not asked me if he could swing by your Pawtucket offices. It seems as if you're trying to invent the wheel before you make the car. You know, or something like that.

One plastic foot is all I need,

David Paulson

264 South Doheny Drive, #8 Beverly Hills, CA 90211

44

CONSUMER AFFAIRS DEPARTMENT

December 17, 2001

MR DAVID PAULSON
264 SOUTH DOHENY DR #8
BEVERLY HILLS, CA 90211

Dear MR PAULSON,

Thank you for contacting us regarding SIMON 2. We appreciate your
bringing this matter to our attention, and we apologize for any
inconvenience this may have caused.

We are very sorry to inform you that the part you requested is not
available separately. We would be glad to assist you with any
further inquiries you may have concerning replacement parts for our
products.

We want to assure you that consumer satisfaction is very important
to us. Please call us at 1-888-836-7025 if we can be of further
assistance.

We look forward to hearing from you soon.

Sincerely,

CONSUMER AFFAIRS DEPT.

Consumer Affairs Representative
10/01/01 891/1B 2958
MEC/mec N9990

August 31, 2001

Southwest Airlines
Customer Relations
P.O. Box 36647 - 1CR
Dallas, Texas 75235-1647

Dear Sir or Madam:

As a constant passenger on your Los Angeles to Oakland run, I have kept a particular question to myself for sometime now. However, frustration has finally gotten the better of me, and I simply must ask. What happened to the honey-roasted peanuts?

All you serve now, are those high in sodium, salted-peanuts. Sure, you give everyone two packets of them, but I'd much rather have one package of honey-roasted peanuts over twelve packages of salted-peanuts. Hell, I'd rather have one package of honey-roasted peanuts over a small Not-For-Resale package of Oreos.

My physician has told me that I have way too much sodium in my diet as it stands, so that's the reason for my being so adamant about the subject at hand. Is there a way to (much like people order Kosher meals prior to take-off) for me to order packages of honey-roasted peanuts instead of salted ones?

Sincerely,

David Paulson

P.S. – I have nothing against Oreos, just in case you guys have anything to do with manufacturing those cookies. But when you're on a plane and don't have a mirror to look into, Oreos are the worst thing to eat... you end up with black speckles wedged in throughout your smile.

---

264 South Doheny Drive, #8 Beverly Hills, CA 90211

SOUTHWEST AIRLINES CO.

Paula Berg
Representative
Customer Relations

Love Field
P.O. Box 36647
Dallas, TX 75235-1611
(214) 792-4762

November 16, 2001   222565

Mr. David Paulson
264 South Doheny Drive #8
Beverly Hills, CA 90211

Dear Mr. Paulson:

Thank you for your letter of August 31. I am sorry to learn of your disappointment with our onboard peanut selection. As a frequent flyer myself, I have often wondered, "What happened to the honey roasted peanuts?"

I too prefer honey roasted to just plain old salted nuts and can certainly understand your dilemma. Typically, we rotate the types of peanuts we serve from honey roasted to salted roasted on a semi-annual. However, in an effort to cut costs following the events of September 11, we will be holding off on honey roasted peanuts until at least the end of the year. Of course, our Customers are always welcome to carry their "goodies of choice" onboard with them, and I have taken the liberty of enclosing a couple of bags for you to take along on your next trip.

Thanks for taking the time to share your thoughts with us. Your business is truly appreciated, and we will look forward to serving you honey roasted peanuts again in the future.

Sincerely,

Paula Berg

/pb/tm

Enclosure: Honey Roasted Peanuts

47

November 6, 2001

Southwest Airlines
Customer Relations
P.O. Box 36647 - 1CR
Dallas, Texas 75235-1647

Dear Sir or Madam:

Since the tragic events of 9/11, airports have obviously ramped up their security measures along with airlines such as yours. Now, airlines are confiscating passenger's corkscrews, pocket knives, hairpins, and tweezers.

As one of those unfortunate individuals that must go through life with what people call a "uni-brow", I am a slave to my tweezers, constantly plunking and yanking unwanted hairs in order to keep that "clean-cut" look I'm so known for. In a normal world, this would be laborious enough, but with your current security measures, it has caused an additional problem.

I plan on flying Southwest to Seattle, Washington during the holiday months so that I may meet my fiancée's parents for the first time ever. As the flight and travel time will clock in at more than 4 hours, any hair that I have plucked from my eyebrows (pre-trip) will most likely grow back as stubble during my traveling. As my fiancée's parents will be waiting at the gate to meet me, I find that my first impression will not be as impressive as I would like it to be, having a stubbly "uni-brow" and all.

I wondered if it may be possible, just this once, to allow me to carry my pair of tweezers on your flight, so that I may keep myself "clean and prepared" for this first time meeting. It would be greatly appreciated and a lifesaver!

Sincerely,

David Paulson

P.S. – The only other option I could think of, assuming the above scenario is not acceptable, is that Southwest provide a Flight Attendant with a pair of tweezers so she can pluck the unwanted hair minutes before I exit the plane at my destination. It might prove to be difficult, as I know my eyebrow lines much better than a stranger, but I would be amenable to that option.

264 South Doheny Drive, #8 Beverly Hills, CA 90211

SOUTHWEST

SOUTHWEST AIRLINES CO.

Betty Bogart
Specialist
Executive Office Customer Communications

Love Field
P.O. Box 36611
Dallas, TX 75235-1611
(214) 792-4966

December 13, 2001   237010

Mr. David Paulson
264 South Doheny Drive, #8
Beverly Hills, California 90211

Dear Mr. Paulson:

Your letter arrived in the Executive Office on November 14, and I hope that this reply arrives in time to facilitate your Holiday travel to meet your future in-laws.

In the days immediately following our return to business on September 14, federal security directives excluded some smaller, cosmetic-type items from carryon luggage, including tweezers. (Incidentally, the same restrictions apply to our Employees as to our Customers, and even our Flight Attendants were unable to carry tweezers onboard the aircraft at one point.) However, I am glad to inform you that federal directives no longer prohibit folks from packing a small set of tweezers in their carryon luggage.

So, this solves your dilemma of making a good first impression on your fiancée's parents. Here's hoping that it's an enjoyable and festive occasion that will pave the way for a lifetime of happy memories.

Sincerely,

Betty Bogart

Betty Bogart

/bb

Copy to: Executive Planning Committee
             Jim Ruppel, Vice President Customer Relations & Rapid Rewards
             Greg Wells, Vice President Safety, Security, and Flight Dispatch
             Teresa Laraba, Senior Director Ground Operations Training &
                 System Projects
             Lisa Anderson, Director Customer Advocacy

November 5, 2001

Scripps Howard National Spelling Bee
312 Walnut Street, 28th Floor
Cincinnati, OH 45202

Dear Sir or Madam:

After some resaerch on your website, it has come to my atention that you have no plans to hold a Spelling Bee competition here in the city of angels, Los Angeles. And that, my letter chalenging friends, is exactly the reason I'm writing!

As a meek child growing up in rurel Nebraska, I can tell you that I was a young adult with little to no courage, constantly questoning my abilities and talents. That is, until Ms. Harper at the Cook Elementary School held her own version of your spelling bee.

I'll never forget the moment that changed my life forever. The word given to me was "dismemberment". I stood up, proudly, having studied my practice book the night before and spelled it. D, I, S, M, E, M, B, R, E, M, E, N, T. Unfortunitely, I was incorect and was forced to leave the competition. But it provided me a thick shell, which I would use over and over again throughout the years, protecting my psychie from a barage of depressing and horific experiences.

Thus my interest in creating a spelling bee for the downtroden here in Los Angeles. I think (and hope) you will agree. Please let me know when I can get started, as the officiale date for the bee, is rapidly aproaching.

Busy as a bee,

David Paulson

264 South Doheny Drive, #8 Beverly Hills, CA 90211

312 WALNUT ST. 28th FLOOR
CINCINNATI, OHIO 45202

www.spellingbee.com   E-mail · bee@scripps.com

November 12, 2001

David Paulson
264 South Doheny Drive, #8
Beverly Hills, CA 90211

Dear Mr. Paulson,

Thank you for your interest in the Scripps Howard National Spelling Bee program.
Sponsorship is available to daily and weekly newspapers serving English-speaking
populations around the world. Each sponsor organizes a spelling bee program in its
community, usually with the cooperation of area school officials. The champion of the
sponsor's final spelling bee advances to the national finals in Washington, D.C.

The *Los Angeles Daily News* sponsors portions of Los Angeles County. For details
regarding their bee program, please contact Lisa Williams, Spelling Bee Coordinator
for the *Los Angeles Daily News*, (818) 713-3517.

Enclosed please find a copy of our *2002 Paideia* study booklet. The *Paideia* is
published annually and contains over 3700 words grouped into 29 categories. For
study tips, activities, and general information about the national program, you may also
wish to visit our web site, www.spellingbee.com.

Sincerely,

Cybelle Weeks
Administrative Assistant

Enclosure

SCRIPPS HOWARD
NATIONAL SPELLING BEE

Headquarters Office Phone · 513 977 3040   Non-Sponsor Orders Only · 1 800 NSB WORD
Headquarters Office Fax · 513 977 3090   Fax Non-Sponsor Orders Only · 1 800 990 6266

51

December 11, 2001

Ms. Lisa Williams
Spelling Bee Coordinator
The Los Angeles Daily News
21221 Oxnard Street
Woodland Hills, CA 91367

Dear Ms. Williams:

Per my correspondence with Cybelle Weeks at The Scripps Howard National Spelling Bee offices, I am contacting you with a small request.

As I am a lover of all things that involve letters, and stringing them together in order to form strange new words and phrases, I originaly contact Ms. Weeks in an attempt to create my own local (Los Angeles based) spelling bee for underpriviledged children and their school-chums. Since your particuler paper has not publicized or put much marketing muscle behind your Bee, I was unaware that you were the Coordinator for this area.

Now that I've found you, I wanted to ask if you'd be ameniable to letting me plan the Spelling Bee out here with you. As for qualifications, I do quite well at Scrabble (the game), and I'm a natural-born leader with leadership qualities that some people say rival the famous General Paton. Of course, I'm aware he's only a fictitious character, but if he was real he'd be the guy you'd say I reminded you of.

My proposel for a Los Angeles based Spelling Bee consists of a few elements I believe you have yet to integrate. From a karaoke-style singing round, where contestants sing out the correct spellings, cued by on-screen asisstance, to a round sponsored by the classic learning game "Speak n' Spell"...I'm full of ideas and a lust for life, something I'm sure has been sucked from your being over many years of planning the same 'ol thing.

Please let me know ASAP if this is all up to snuff. Otherwise, I'd like to start going on my own Spelling Bee which I'd hold in early February. I've already talked to the Principal of Beverly Hills High, who will let me hold it there assuming I have the National organization's "John Hancock".

S,I,N,C,E,R,L,Y,

David Paulson

264 South Doheny Drive, #8 Beverly Hills, CA 90211

September 28, 2001

American Egg Board
1460 Renaissance Drive
Park Ridge, Illinois 60068

Dear Sir or Madam:

Are you still referring to our white, oval friends as "the incredible, edible egg?" If so, I'd love to know what's so gosh darn incredible about them. I mean, please, I see them everywhere.

On a totally different note – when do these "edible eggs" transform from chicken embryos to actual food items?

Sincerely,

David Paulson

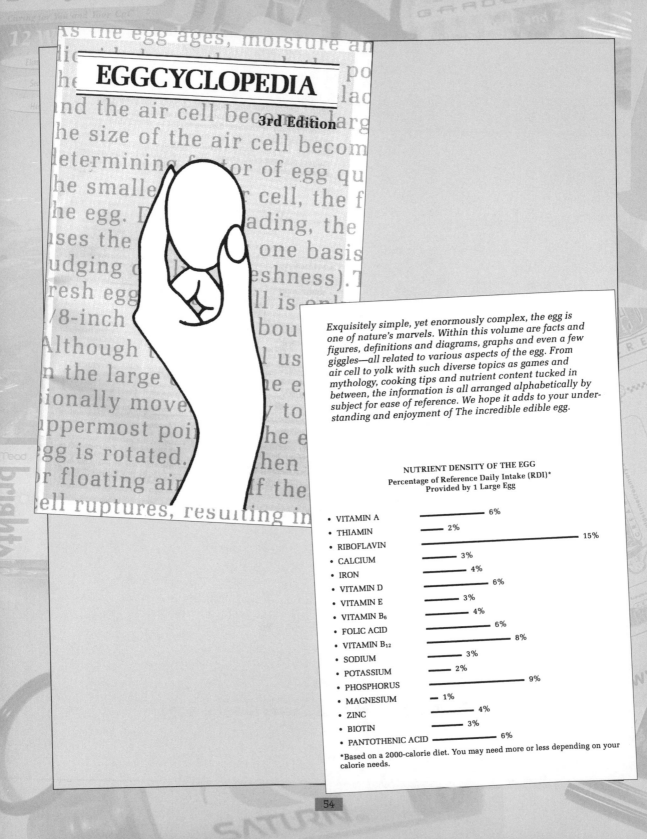

EGGCYCLOPEDIA

3rd Edition

(background text, partially obscured:) s the egg ages, moisture an... po... and the air cell bec... larg... he size of the air cell becom... determining factor of egg qu... he smaller... cell, the f... he egg. D... ading, the... uses the... one basis... udging o... eshness). T... resh egg... ll is on... /8-inch... bou... Although... us... n the large... e e... sionally move... y to... ppermost poi... he e... egg is rotated... hen... or floating ai... f the... cell ruptures, resulting in...

Exquisitely simple, yet enormously complex, the egg is one of nature's marvels. Within this volume are facts and figures, definitions and diagrams, graphs and even a few giggles—all related to various aspects of the egg. From air cell to yolk with such diverse topics as games and mythology, cooking tips and nutrient content tucked in between, the information is all arranged alphabetically by subject for ease of reference. We hope it adds to your understanding and enjoyment of The incredible edible egg.

NUTRIENT DENSITY OF THE EGG
Percentage of Reference Daily Intake (RDI)*
Provided by 1 Large Egg

Nutrient	% RDI
• VITAMIN A	6%
• THIAMIN	2%
• RIBOFLAVIN	15%
• CALCIUM	3%
• IRON	4%
• VITAMIN D	6%
• VITAMIN E	3%
• VITAMIN B$_6$	4%
• FOLIC ACID	6%
• VITAMIN B$_{12}$	8%
• SODIUM	3%
• POTASSIUM	2%
• PHOSPHORUS	9%
• MAGNESIUM	1%
• ZINC	4%
• BIOTIN	3%
• PANTOTHENIC ACID	6%

*Based on a 2000-calorie diet. You may need more or less depending on your calorie needs.

December 10, 2001

American Egg Board
1460 Renaissance Drive
Park Ridge, Illinois 60068

Dear Sir or Madam:

On September 28th, I wrote you a letter asking if you were still referring to our white, oval friends as "the incredible, edible egg?" Your response was simply to send me a booklet entitled, "Eggcyclopedia" and leave it at that.

Unfortunately, this "Eggcyclopedia" did not answer my question, but further enraged me that you would dare send me a booklet about eggs, of all things! I mean, is this how you handle your customers? Is this how an American Egg Board handles business? Simply ship off a packet of paper, further killing the Amazon Rain Forests, in a lazy attempt at making someone else do the work? For people associated with hard-boiled goodness, I find it hard to believe.

So, I ask you again. Are you still referring to our white, oval friends as "the incredible, edible egg?"

Sincerely,

David Paulson

---

264 South Doheny Drive, #8 Beverly Hills, CA 90211

September 17, 2001

M&M/Mars, Inc.
Customer Service Dept. (Re: Skittles)
Hackettstown, NJ 07840-1503

Dear Sir or Madam:

I recently purchased a package of your Sour Skittles, and was faced with what I believe to be quite a surprise – you replaced your Lime flavored Skittles with Green Apple!

Upon closer inspection of the package, I realized that this change was not by accident. In fact, the front of the package (which I'm including just so you know I wasn't making this up), asked for my opinion as a consumer, on whether or not I felt you should "Keep the Apple", and "Lose the Lime".

Here's the way I look at it. Lime is a traditional flavor. It's included in food products such as soda, other chewy candies (which I won't mention out of respect for your company), cookies, underarm deodorants (it's true!), and various other drinks and condiments. But Green Apple? It's a much rarer flavor in today's world! I can only think of one or two items that use it, and that was after pondering the subject for at least an hour.

So, honestly, it comes down to one thing. Is M&M/Mars looking to evolve into a candy company that takes risks (i.e. going with Green Apple), or wants to continue along the pathway of the status quo (i.e. staying with Lime). And on top of that, does M&M/Mars really want to show its consumers that it knows so little about candy (i.e. asking consumers what they think), by asking them what they should do next? Of course, the latter is a problem you've already thrust yourselves into, but like my Uncle Murphy always said, "You gotta take the good, you gotta take the bad, you gotta take it all, and then you sit down and have a scotch and it'll all be clear." And so, in memory of Uncle Murphy, I think you're doing the right thing.

As for Green Apple or Lime, I say you keep the Lime. It's more familiar. It complements the other flavors in Sour Skittles, and it's totally one-hundred percent American. And with this week's sad events, the last thing you want to do is stick a foreign flavor into an All-American product.

As I'm sure you appreciate my opinion, I'd appreciate your thoughts on my thoughts in this matter.

God Bless America,

David Paulson

264 South Doheny Drive, #8 Beverly Hills, CA 90211

a division of Mars, Incorporated
High Street, Hackettstown, New Jersey 07840 • Telephone 908-852-1000

October 1, 2001

Hi Mr. David Paulson,

Thank you for your letter and your interest in our Green Apples Madness promotion.

This promotion has ended and lime was the winning flavor! This flavor will be back in packages very soon.

Sincerely,

Robin G. Criss
Consumer Affairs

RGC/cl 4250153A

October 7, 2001

Ms. Robin G. Criss
Consumer Affairs
M&M/Mars, Inc.
High Street
Hackettstown, NJ 07840-1503

Dear Ms. Criss:

You can imagine my excitement upon hearing that M&M/Mars has decided to return the LIME flavor back into packages of your Sour Skittles.

Whether or not you remember, my thoughts were that "you keep the Lime." That it was "more familiar" and was "totally one-hundred percent American". I am extremely glad that my thoughts and the thoughts of M&M/Mars are on the same page. In fact, I would be more than happy to be your "ace in the hole" when it comes to re-thinking your candy packaging. You could, quite possibly, keep me on retainer for the "tough decisions". Just an idea, but it struck me as being a good one for M&M/Mars. Did I mention I was pretty cheap, too?

I did have one piece of advice for you, Ms. Criss. When replying to a consumer's letter, the least you can do is actually WRITE one. The reply you sent me looked like you cut and pasted the text from a "form e-mail" that you had sent before, then hastily pasted your name at the bottom. Sure, I bet it saved you some time, but do we really need to be saving time and cutting corners when it has to do with consumers? I think not.

On that note, I hope that you can at least respond to this letter with an actual reply, instead of sending me a letter you've previously sent to a hundred other people across this great country of ours.

On retainer, if you need me to be,

David Paulson

264 South Doheny Drive, #8 Beverly Hills, CA 90211

October 2, 2001

Mr. Barry Shepard
Star-Kist Foods, Inc.
A subsidiary of the H.J. Heinz Company
P.O. Box 57
Pittsburgh, PA 15230-0057
Attn: Corporate Affairs Department

Dear Mr. Shepard:

As the Vice President of Marketing (congratulations, by the way), I'm sure you're extremely aware of consumers' thoughts and desires when it comes to purchasing a quality tuna product. I mean that's why you have the job you have, right?

Over the last decade, I have found myself extremely amused by your television ads, especially the ones including the loveable and wry character, CHARLIE the TUNA. I mean, let's be honest, this guy should have his own feature-length movie! You may want to talk to PIXAR, the company that created Toy Story and A Bug's Life, before someone else steals your idea to center a movie around a charismatic and verbose tuna like him.

Based on CHARLIE the TUNA's appeal, however, I find it's now hard to stomach your tuna. I mean, you're advertising the food I'm about to eat, using a loveable creature who just happens to be the food I'm about to chomp down on!! That's like having a cow on the TV ads for McDonald's. (And you don't see them doing that, do you?)

I wanted to appeal to your sense of love for all creatures of the sea, in seriously thinking about changing your mascot. What about an older man, like someone's grandfather, who can hail the positives of your product? Or what about a dolphin? The dolphin could even say something like, "I provide a home for these loveable tunas in my stomach, and when asked nicely, give it up to the great people at Star-Kist. And they don't hurt me, either!". (You could silence all those dolphin-safe tuna people with that commercial, as well.)

Until you do so, I find that it's going to be hard to stomach your tuna product. Although mayonnaise helps a little, It still can't erase the memory of CHARLIE the TUNA. And it's not just me, Mr. Shepard... There's already a newsgroup on the Internet that has been created (alt.food.mascots), where individuals have already been complaining.

What do you think we can do about this?

Kindest regards,

David Paulson

_____

264 South Doheny Drive, #8 Beverly Hills, CA 90211

Heinz U.S.A., Division of H. J. Heinz Company
StarKist Seafood, Division of Star-Kist Foods, Inc.
Heinz Pet Products, Division of Star-Kist Foods, Inc.

1062 Progress Street
Pittsburgh, Pennsylvania 15212-5990
Telephone: 412 237 5757

November 5, 2001

Mr. David Paulson
264 South Doheny Drive #8
Beverly Hills, CA 90211

Dear Mr. Paulson:

Thank you for your letter to Barry Shepard, Vice President of Marketing, regarding Charlie the Tuna. Please accept my apology for the delay in responding.

We appreciate your interest in Charlie the Tuna and are glad you've enjoyed seeing Charlie in recent StarKist commercials. To date, we haven't attempted to place Charlie the Tuna as a central character in a feature film; however, you'll be pleased to learn that Charlie will be a star in the upcoming movie "Foodfight" scheduled to be released late next summer.

In terms of your attachment to Charlie, and resulting reluctance to enjoy a nutritious, tasty meal of StarKist Tuna, maybe it will help to remember that while Charlie appeared in his first StarKist television commercial in 1961, he still hasn't done everything he needs to in order to meet StarKist's high-quality standards for great-tasting tuna. So we hope you'll take comfort in the fact that "StarKist doesn't want tuna with good taste, StarKist wants tuna that tastes good!"

We have no plans to retire Charlie the Tuna at this time, Mr. Paulson. We hope you will remain a satisfied StarKist consumer, and we appreciate your comments.

Sincerely,

Carla Dundes
General Manager, Consumer Affairs

September 27, 2001

President & CEO
SKECHERS USA, Inc.
228 Manhattan Beach Blvd.
Manhattan Beach, CA 90266

Dear Sir or Madam:

Every time I see your commercials, I have to wonder aloud just exactly what the name
SKECHERS stands for.

I always thought it was simply the phonetic spelling of the sound that your shoes make as
they scrape across the concrete sidewalks. However, my second cousin Lilly, who is one
of those Generation-X kids with her tattoos and colored hair had told me it was a
Norwegian word that means, "one with a penchant for walking upright", and that sort of
seemed to make sense.

Well, which one is it?

Sincerely,

David Paulson

---

264 South Doheny Drive, #8 Beverly Hills, CA 90211

SKECHERS U.S.A.
F O O T W E A R

October 8, 2001

Mr. David Paulson
264 S. Doheny Dr., #8
Beverly Hills, CA 90211

Dear Mr. Paulson,

Thank you for your recent letter to us asking about the meaning of the name "SKECHERS".

The definition of a "SKECHER" is someone who can't sit still, and who always needs to know how they look and who is image – conscious and trendy. This definition came from the surf world and as we say in L.A. "the Valley". It also refers to someone who may be high maintenance with regards to their personal fashion.

I hope that sheds some light on what our name means to us, we like your definitions too!

Sincerely,

SKECHERS USA

December 11, 2001

SKECHERS USA, Inc.
228 Manhattan Beach Blvd.
Manhattan Beach, CA 90266

Dear Sir or Madam:

Thank you for your letter dated October 8th in which you shed some light on just what the name SKECHERS means. I was somewhat happy to hear that you liked my definition as well: *"One with a penchant for walking upright"*.

That's why I immediately set forth in creating what I call "The Penchant Uprights". Hilarious at times, often taking stabs at pop-culture, and one-hundred percent animated – "The Penchant Uprights" is a crazy animated TV pilot sponsored by, who else… SKECHERS USA, Inc.!

Based on your friendly assistance, I also saw fit to include a character in the family of Uprights named "Skechermanic Sketch". Don't ask me what his name means, but doesn't it just reek of excitement and energy? I think so, too.

Now, all I need from you and your superiors, is a letter stating that SKECHERS USA, Inc., is attached as the official sponsor of the program. Once I have that, I think the doors will start to open. I'm thinking the WB first, then maybe FOX or UPN. If you have any thoughts or want to come with me (wearing your Skechers of course), I'd be happy to accommodate you.

Let me know if I should have my copyright lawyer Sid Blankman give you a ring, or if you'd like to sit down with me first.

Walking upright,

David Paulson

264 South Doheny Drive, #8 Beverly Hills, CA 90211

October 2, 2001

President & CEO
SC Johnson
1525 Howe Street
Racine, Wisconsin 53403-5011

Dear Sir or Madam:

As an avid food re-heater and freezer, I find that I use your product more often than you may have expected normal consumers to use it. I re-package food at least seven to ten times a day, storing them away in your famous ZIPLOC brand baggies.

However, as a color-blind individual, I find that I cannot take advantage of your clever, "blue and yellow make green" feature. For the life of me, however hard I try to concentrate on the colored plastic rims, I just can't make the color green show up. Obviously this isn't your fault – it's mine. But some say, you've just got to live with what God's given you, and move on.

I did wonder, however, if possibly there was a way to re-imagine your "blue and yellow make green" baggies for those who are color blind? What about, "rough edge and smooth edge make a rough/smooth edge"? Or how about, "small dotted line and long dashy line make small dotted lines and long dashy lines"? I know, I'm not an idea man, but it's got to be a start.

I appeal to your goodwill and your support of all types of consumers, and hope that you may find a way to grace my eyes with a special-edition ZIPLOC bag.

Kindest regards,

David Paulson

---

264 South Doheny Drive, #8 Beverly Hills, CA 90211

SC Johnson

A FAMILY COMPANY

S. C. Johnson & Son, Inc.
1525 Howe Street
Racine, WI 53403-2236
262.260.2000

October 26, 2001

Mr. David Paulson
264 S Doheny Drive #8
Beverly Hills, CA 90211

Dear Mr. Paulson:

Thank you for contacting us.

Like most companies that manufacture retail products, we receive many suggestions from individuals who are not employees. We appreciate the thoughtfulness which prompts these suggestions. To avoid misunderstanding, we have adopted a uniform policy for handling and evaluating them.

Ideas relating to new products, processes, packages or product improvements will be considered only if the suggestion is submitted in writing along with the attached Suggestion Agreement and Release form.

If you would like to submit your suggestion, please complete and sign the enclosed form. Attach a brief description of your idea to one copy and mail it to us. (Keep the other copy for yourself.) A postage-paid return label is enclosed for your use.

As soon as we receive and review the requested information, we will contact you.

Sincerely,

Jacquelynn

Jacquelynn K. Johnson
Consumer Liability Specialist
Consumer Resource Center

Questions? Please call 1-800-558-5252 and provide your reference number: 5223700A.

December 2, 2001

Ms. Jacquelynn K. Johnson
Consumer Liability Specialist
SC Johnson Consumer Resource Center
1525 Howe Street
Racine, Wisconsin 53403-5011

Reference Number: 5223700A

Dear Ms. Johnson:

Sorry it's taken me so long to respond to your letter dated October 26th, 2001. As you can imagine, I've been on the road testing my prototype Ziploc baggies for the color blind at malls across this great country of ours. As I'm sure you may or may not know, finding individuals afflicted with the "color blindness" is about as easy as finding a needle in a haystack. But I trudge on.

Enclosed you will find the "Suggestion Agreement and Release" for my product which I originally wrote to you about. In a nutshell, Ziploc bags that do not require the "yellow and blue makes green" mechanism to confirm a tightly closed bag. Instead, my trademark "rough edge and smooth edge make a rough/smooth edge", along with my "small dotted line and long dashy line make small dotted lines and long dashy lines", will revolutionize the world of storage bags for the colorly-inclined.

On a totally unrelated note, I wondered if you could (under the table) provide me with a stipend so that I may continue my testing and research. I've been wanting to do some testing at The Mall of America, but I just don't have the cash for a round trip ticket. And let's be honest – who wants to get stranded at The Mall of America with the crowds of in-bred families and their pet rocks. Not me, no sir.

I look forward to hearing from you regarding the stipend.

Kindest regards,

David Paulson
Inventor, Ziploc Bags For The Colorly-Inclined

264 South Doheny Drive, #8 Beverly Hills, CA 90211

SC Johnson
A FAMILY COMPANY

S. C. Johnson & Son, Inc.
1525 Howe Street
Racine, Wisconsin 53403-2235

e 04

SUGGESTION AGREEMENT AND RELEASE

Attention: **Patent Department**

I wish to submit to S. C. Johnson & Son, Inc., and/or its subsidiaries (hereinafter "JOHNSON"), for its evaluation my suggestion which ☐ is attached ☑ was previously sent with my letter of

Oct 2nd, 20 _01_, relating to _Ziploc containers for color blind people_

I understand that JOHNSON has established a uniform policy regarding its evaluation of suggestions offered by persons outside its organization. In accordance with such policy, I agree to the following conditions:

1. JOHNSON does not solicit suggestions, but is willing to consider the suggestion of a person outside its organization, at the request of the suggestor.

2. I acknowledge that this disclosure and any related future disclosure made by me is NOT MADE IN CONFIDENCE and NO CONFIDENTIAL RELATIONSHIP exists now or will exist in the future between me and JOHNSON.

3. In consideration of JOHNSON'S evaluation of my suggestion, I hereby RELEASE JOHNSON from any liability in connection with the adoption or use of my suggestion except such liability as may arise under valid patents, now or hereafter issued, or under a formal written contract, if such is hereafter made.

4. No obligation of any kind is assumed by nor may any obligations be implied against JOHNSON, unless and until a formal written contract has been made, and then the obligation shall be only as is expressed in such formal written contract.

5. By requesting consideration of my suggestion, I do not grant to JOHNSON any rights under any existing patent or patents which may later be obtained covering my suggestion.

6. All disclosures must be submitted in writing, and JOHNSON assumes no responsibility for the return of any written description, photographs, drawings, models or samples which may be submitted.

7. THIS AGREEMENT sets forth my entire understanding with JOHNSON and supersedes any previous discussions or correspondence regarding the subject matter I am now disclosing.

I have carefully read this Agreement and agree to the above conditions and ask you to consider my above-entitled suggestion under these conditions.

Signed _David Paulsen_ (SEAL)

Address _264 S. Doheny Dr. #8_
_BH, CA 90211_

Distribution: *(Separate copies)*

White: Send to S. C. Johnson & Son, Inc. (Mail Sta. 039)

Yellow: **CONSUMER's copy ---- ‖ KEEP YELLOW COPY FOR YOUR FILE ‖**

67

SC **Johnson**

A FAMILY COMPANY

S. C. Johnson & Son, Inc.
1525 Howe Street
Racine, WI 53403-2236
262.260.2000

July 25, 2002

Mr. David Paulson
264 South Doheny Drive, #8
Beverly Hills, CA 90211

Dear Mr. Paulson:

Thank you for your signed Suggestion Agreement and Release offering an unsolicited idea. While we appreciate the thoughtfulness which prompts this suggestion, we have no interest in this concept at this time.

We are unable to offer you a stipend to continue your consumer work. S. C. Johnson conducts its consumer testing through established consumer panels.

However, thank you, again, for the interest you have expressed in our company.

Very truly yours,

S. C. JOHNSON & SON, INC.

Donna M. Mooney
Law Department

/dm

dmm2044-6

October 26, 2001

The Discovery Communications, Inc.
7700 Wisconsin Avenue
Bethesda, MD 20814-3579
Attn: Discovery Store Consumer Assistance

Dear Sir or Madam:

During a recent visit to one of your NATURE COMPANY stores, (which may now go by a different name, although I'm pretty sure it was called that when I was last there), I realized that you no longer carried your "Scorpion encased in a plastic cube" product.

Having just come back from a trip to Egypt with a group of friends, I have to tell you that I was extremely excited to get back to the United States and purchase a whole bunch of your "Scorpion encased in a plastic cube" product. Since a few of my friends on the trip to Egypt (Jamie, Brian, and Frank) all came dangerously close to being stung and killed by scorpions, I thought "How great would it be to put a lifesize, authentic looking scorpion in their bathtub or tropical drink!!" Of course, The Nature Company no longer carries such a product.

I wondered if you have chosen to stop carrying your "Scorpion encased in a plastic cube" product for any particular reason, or if it will be coming back soon to your stores. If so, please let me know where and when so I can purchase a whole bunch of them.

Best regards,

David Paulson

264 South Doheny Drive, #8 Beverly Hills, CA 90211

Viewer Relations
P.O. Box 665
Florence, KY 41022

1-888-404-5969
Fax 859-727-8918
viewer_relations@discovery.com

David Paulson
264 South Doheny Drive
Beverly Hills, CA 90211

November 13, 2001

Dear Mr. Paulson:

Thank you for contacting *Discovery Channel* and taking the time to write to us with your comments about the "scorpion in a plastic cube" product. Unfortunately, we do not have any information on exactly why this product is no longer carried within our stores and we do not expect it back at this time. *Discovery Channel* purchased the *Nature Company* within the last two years and has replaced a number of their stores with *Discovery Channel* stores. We recommend searching the Internet for this item so that you can trick your friends.

In the future, if you have a question about airdates, want to purchase home videos, or would like to see some of the items we carry now, we invite you to visit our website at www.discovery.com.

Thank you for taking the time to write us with your thoughts about our products.

Sincerely,
Discovery Networks
Viewer Relations

590110/tb

NETWORKS OF DISCOVERY COMMUNICATIONS, INC.

October 4, 2001

Radio Shack Corporation
200 Taylor Street, Suite 600
Ft. Worth, TX 76102
Attn: Customer Relations

Dear Sir or Madam:

About three weeks ago I happened to be in your Radio Shack store looking for some cable TV cords for my new TIVO. I don't know if you've heard of TIVO, but it allows you to record programs when you're not at home, then watch them at a totally different time than when the program originally aired! It's quite honestly the most amazing technology to come around since eight-track tapes... but I digress.

On the particular day in question, while I was perusing your extensive collection of cable TV cords, I heard a certain "PSST" coming from behind me. There, standing behind me, was a strange old-looking woman who was holding a five dollar bill in her hand. She quickly shoved it into my pocket (which was alarming and exciting all at the same time), and ran out of the store. When I turned around, I saw a clerk of yours on the phone, and the cash register open wide.

In putting two and two together, I believe this nice-looking old woman, in fact, had stolen the five dollars from your open register while your clerk was on the phone. And thus, I have enclosed this five dollar bill, so it may be returned to the Radio Shack bank account and gain the interest your corporation needs to continue serving up the best cable TV cords and antennas that the world has to offer.

You may wonder, of course, why it has taken me three weeks to return the money to you. And quite honestly, I have to say that there was a moment there where I was unsure I was going to return the money. Five dollars, you know, can buy an awful lot of bean burritos at TACO BELL. Hell, I could have eaten there for a week on that cash. But when it came down to it, Mexican food simply paled in comparison to doing a generous deed, that quite possibly, could result in an even bigger reward from yours truly!

Kindest and most generous regards,

David Paulson

Enclosure:
$5 Dollar Bill

---

264 South Doheny Drive, #8 Beverly Hills, CA 90211

December 11, 2001

Radio Shack Corporation
200 Taylor Street, Suite 600
Ft. Worth, TX 76102
Attn: Customer Relations

Dear Sir or Madam:

In early October I drafted a letter to your company, informing you that I had been handed a five dollar bill by an elderly customer in your Los Angeles store that I had believed was stolen from an open cash register. I went so far as to send your company (to the above address) the actual five dollar bill in an attempt to be honest, without trying to turn the situation into something advantageous for myself. But alas, two months later, I still have received no thank you, no gift certificate, no T-shirts or electronic gifts in my mailbox.

You know, if you expect people to be honest in this society, especially in your stores, the least you could do is send people some kind of certificate that proclaims how cool they are when they do something selfless. And if you can't do that, I want that five dollars back!

Please inform me of how you wish to proceed. My lawyer, who just happens to be the guy who represented that guy who stole that car and was on the run from cops on the Los Angeles freeway for like twenty-two hours, is my lawyer too. And can I just say, what is it with these people who race away from cops? I mean, c'mon, we all know how those things end. With a spike strip, that's how.

Kindest and most generous regards,

David Paulson

264 South Doheny Drive, #8 Beverly Hills, CA 90211

RadioShack.
C O R P O R A T I O N

200 Taylor Street, Suite 600
Fort Worth, Texas 76102
Phone 817-415-8776
FAX 817-415-3240

December 20, 2001

DAVID PAULSON
264 S DOHENY DR #8
BEVERLY HILLS, CA 90211

Dear Mr. Paulson:

Please accept our apologies for the delay in responding to your letter dated
December 11, 2001.

We did receive your $5.00 bill late in October. Regretfully, your letter was
misplaced before we could respond to it. After checking with our Accounting
Assistant, I was provided with a copy of the receipt for these monies, which I
have attached to this letter.

With our sincerest appreciation for being honest in sending us these monies, we
are sending you two $10.00 "Customer Appreciation Dollars" that can be used
on your next visit to RadioShack.

We at RadioShack wish you and your family a "Happy Holiday Season".

Sincerely,

Rose Funari

Rose Funari
Customer Care Center

Enclosures

December 27, 2001

Ms. Rose Funari
Customer Care Center
Radio Shack Corporation
200 Taylor Street, Suite 600
Ft. Worth, TX 76102

Dear Ms. Funari:

Twenty dollars. Two words that rang out in my head over and over again as I held the "Customer Appreciation Dollars" that you most generously sent me on December 20, 2001. In a single moment, my faith in your corporation's generosity was instilled once again. And in the moment after that, I realized how stupid you guys really are.

Think about it. Some customer from the middle of nowhere sends you five dollars. Tells you he found it in your store. Wants some kind of recognition. What do you do? Send him back <u>twenty</u> <u>dollars</u>! That's a fifteen dollar loss to the Radio Shack Corporation. And assuming you do this fairly often, you're single-handedly running Radio Shack into the ground. As someone who buys and sells on the stock market, your company is the last corporation I'd invest in. I mean, look at you – you're just giving money away!!

You may want to think about doing what I suggested in my previous letter. Send customers who are honest a "Customer Appreciation Certificate". On it, you could type some old English ode like, "Herein lies a customer with such honesty, integrity, and forthrighteousness, that Radio Shack dubs thee a Customer who has been appreciated with this herein certificate therein." Then you could sign it or something like that. You know, sort of like the Knights of the Round Table or when the Queen of England knights famous singers and movie-stars.

I hope my brief suggestions help you the next time a situation like this arises. Please give my best to your family (if you have one), and if not say hey to your fellow customer care center peeps.

Happy new year,

David Paulson

P.S. – On a totally unrelated note, the product that I'd like to buy with my twenty dollars actually costs around $49.99. Is there any way you could forward me an additional $29.99 in "Customer Appreciation Dollars" as soon as possible so I may purchase it before the prices go up?

---

264 South Doheny Drive, #8 Beverly Hills, CA 90211

October 26, 2001

AAMCO Transmissions
1 Presidential Boulevard
Bala Cynwyd, PA 19004
Attn: Customer Service Department

Dear Sir or Madam:

First of all, I have to say that I love your commercial where the announcer says, "Where you gonna go," and then you hear that person say, "Double A, M, C, O", and then someone honks their horn like two times. It's really great.

Secondly, my car has been making a weird sound lately. When I start it up, it makes a grinding sound of some kind and the oil light comes on. When I try to drive it, which it won't, it continues to make that grinding sound and there's some black smoke coming from the front under the hood. For the life of me, I can't quite figure out what's wrong.

Because it makes that grinding sound, I can't drive it anywhere to get it looked at, and must instead ride the bus, like I have done recently. But riding the bus doesn't fix my car. That's what AAMCO is for, right!?

I'd appreciate it if you could tell me what to do next in the repair of my automobile. I'll remind you once again, that it makes a grinding noise and the oil light comes on. Sometimes there's black smoke, although sometimes the smoke is invisible but smells bad.

Beep beep, yourselves,

David Paulson

---

264 South Doheny Drive, #8 Beverly Hills, CA 90211

World's Largest Transmission Specialists

November 1, 2001

David Paulson
264 S. Doheny Drive
#8
Beverly Hills, CA 90211

Dear Mr. Paulson:

Thank you for contacting our office and allowing us the opportunity to address your needs.

We have discussed your needs with the AAMCO location nearest to your home address. At this time, they have offered for you to bring the vehicle in to get it checked out. The AAMCO center will perform a no charge External Diagnostic Service on your vehicle to determine if there is a transmission problem.

To take advantage of this offer, please contact your nearest local AAMCO center.

Sincerely,

Mariam Davis
Customer Relations Representative

MHD/ck

September 17, 2001

Consumer Affairs
Dr. Pepper/Seven Up, Inc.
P.O. Box 869077
Plano, TX 75086-9077

Dear Sir or Madam:

I recently caught a television commercial for your product on my local station, in which speeding cars on a dangerous freeway smash into an entire 7UP vending machine – sending cans and debris all over the ground.

I don't know if you're aware of how things work in this country, but kids are extremely influential human beings, and often imitate the things they see on television.

Take, for example, the movie Varsity Blues in which a football player lays on the freeway and lets cars drive over him. Weeks into the films' release, a teenager tried this, with fatal results. And let's also not forget the television show, Jackass, in which individuals do stupid stunts often putting them in dangerous, life-threatening situations. Teenagers have followed suit, also hurting themselves in a copy-cat type scenario.

And now 7UP? I find it extremely dangerous for your company to be airing television commercials in which automobiles smash into vending machines. Not to mention, I want to know who in their right mind decided to wheel a vending machine out onto the freeway in the first place!! First of all, that person must have been either really strong, have a group of friends available to help move it out there, or use of a crane of some kind.

On top of all that, this commercial has hit extremely close to home in that my Uncle Brian owns a vending machine company and is responsible for keeping them stocked with sodas and candy. I can only imagine if he was working on one of his vending machines and some kid who saw your commercial decided to smash into it "just for the fun of it." Terrible, terrible stuff.

I personally want to know what you're going to end up doing in regards to this commercial based on my concerns.

Sincerely,

David Paulson

264 South Doheny Drive, #8 Beverly Hills, CA 90211

Dr Pepper/Seven Up, Inc.
Consumer Relations
P.O. Box 869077, Plano, Texas 75086-9077
5301 Legacy Drive, Plano, Texas 75024
800-696-5891

October 2, 2001

Mr. David Paulson
264 S Doney Drive #8
Beverly Hills, CA 90211

Dear Mr. Paulson:

Thank you for contacting Dr Pepper/Seven Up, Inc. about our television commercials.   Your comments and inquiries are appreciated because they give us valuable feedback about our brands.

Your comments will be taken seriously in evaluating future advertisements. We will forward your comments to our Marketing and Advertising departments.

You are our valued customer, and we appreciate you taking the time to advise us of your opinion.

Sincerely,

Consumer Relations Coordinator

December 14, 2001

Fisher-Price
636 Girard Avenue
East Aurora, NY 14052
Attn: Customer Service

Dear Sir or Madam:

I am writing you with a few questions on your product that you call the "Bubblin' Spa Pool".

Having recently found out about the "Bubblin' Spa Pool" after doing a quick search for hot tubs on the Internet, I began to think that purchasing the above product may be a nice alternative to having to spend an arm and a leg on a full-size hot tub. Especially with today's economy how it is, and the stock market faltering, saving money is my primary goal!

Upon checking out the going price for your "Bubblin' Spa Pool", I realized that it only costs $29.99. Quite honestly, I wondered if this happened to be a typo. How can your sell a hot tub to the American public for $29.99!? Do I have to put it together myself? Do I have to go see some real estate presentation before getting one? What's the catch?

My reason for purchasing the "Bubblin' Spa Pool", is so that I may entertain in my backyard and provide my friends the opportunity to "take a dip" and have a few drinks in the hot tub. You know, music playing, food on the BBQ, and nice cold beers – all the while, hanging out in a pot of bubblin' hot water! A dream, quite honestly. A dream, I tell you! But for $29.99, I should probably purchase ten of them while I'm at it! I mean, normal hot tubs, from companies that are obviously out to screw me on the cost, range anywhere from $600.00 to $2000.00 dollars.

Kudos to your company for taking a chance and giving a little bit back to the American public in this time of need! Really, it's greatly appreciated! All I need to know, now, is just what kind of availability there is on this product? Will it be possible for me to take advantage of this great deal and take home ten of these babies?

Stews a cookin',

David Paulson

264 South Doheny Drive, #8 Beverly Hills, CA 90211

December 24, 2001

Mr David Paulson
264 S Doheny Dr #8
Beverly Hills, CA 90211

Dear Mr Paulson:

Thank you for contacting Fisher-Price. We appreciate the opportunity to respond.

We apologize for the misunderstanding regarding our Bubblin' Spa Pool. This is not a hot tub for adults, but rather a small pool for children. The following is a description of this product:

This inflatable pool is really cool, and lots of bubblin' fun! Connect it to your garden hose, turn it on and feel the refreshing jet of bubbles - aah, just like a real spa. Big enough for a party of friends, with a built-in headrest for relaxing. Inflates to 60" diameter, with 15" high walls; maximum water depth 10" (an automatic drain won't let it overfill). Made of soft, durable plastic. It is for children ages 3 and up.

We appreciate the time you took to check with us. If you have any questions or concerns in the future, please feel free to call us at 800-432-5437, Monday - Friday, 8:00 am - 6:00 pm, ET.

Sincerely,

Fisher-Price, Inc.
Consumer Relations

Ref. # 8935012

636 Girard Ave., East Aurora, New York 14052

October 7, 2001

eBay Inc.
2145 Hamilton Avenue
San Jose, CA 95125
Attn: Customer Assistance

Dear Sir or Madam:

Congratulations are in order!! I just read in a magazine that one of the big movie studios is going to be doing a movie that's all about eBay! As a big fan of the site, you can imagine my excitement upon hearing such wonderful news. All you have to hope for now, is that a star like Stallone or Willis or Swartzenegger ends up starring in it! I'll keep my fingers crossed for you guys!

However, the real reason I'm writing, was to get the answer to a particular question that's been gnawing at my brain lately. In fact, I got into a big debate over this question with my neighbor, Bobby – who just happens to be a retired-jockey who gave up the horse racing for a glass of bourbon. What can I say, everyone's got their vices.

What Bobby and I would like to know is, why can't people auction off body parts and/or internal organs on eBay?

According to the law, if it's my personal lung that I want to auction off, or perhaps my liver – these are organs that I own. They're mine. Just as I can choose whether or not to give them away when I die, shouldn't I be allowed to do so via an online auction service?

Bobby seems to think that the reason behind your company "not allowing" this practice to occur, stems from the fact that eBay can't confirm whether or not these body parts are "high in quality". Meaning, you just don't know whether it's a pristine liver or one that's been abused over the years, and normal everyday consumers just don't know how to tell the difference. I mean, there's no Consumer Reports out there that can help you decide which lung you should purchase. Is that why?

Either way, I'd love to know the answer, as I've got fifteen dollars riding on it.

An auction a day...

David Paulson

---

264 South Doheny Drive, #8 Beverly Hills, CA 90211

eBay Inc.

173 West Election Road

Draper, Utah 84020

Phone 801-619-2400

Fax 801-619-0467

www.ebay.com

David Paulson
264 South Doheny Drive #8
Beverly Hills CA 90211

October 24, 2001

Dear David,

Thank you for taking the time to write to us concerning our policy regarding human parts and remains.

The eBay policy prohibiting the sale of human body parts is based on a number of factors. Primarily, our policies are often designed to protect eBay members from entering into transactions that pose potential legal problems or may be outright illegal. As you can imagine, the sale of items such as this would be illegal or at the least highly regulated. With this in mind, eBay policy often errs on the side of caution by prohibiting items that may be legal to sell but which are questionable in nature.

We feel that policies such as this are important in the long run to protect not only eBay members, but also eBay itself from problems that may arise as a result of permitting these types of transactions.

I hope this information is what you were looking for. I also share in your excitement for our site and our community and hope that you continue to enjoy it.

Regards,

eBay Community Watch Team

December 11, 2001

eBay Community Watch Team
c/o eBay Inc.
2145 Hamilton Avenue
San Jose, CA 95125

Dear Sir or Madam:

In your letter dated October 24th, you outline eBay's policy regarding the auctioning off of human body parts and remains. But I still have a few questions, which I'm sure you have the answers to.

1. Can I auction off my dog's liver? I mean, he's not human so it doesn't fall under the policy regarding "human parts and remains."

2. Is it possible to auction off a "stuffed animal", such as a Moose head, and/or a stuffed cat or dog? These are, of course, remains – but it "remains" to be seen whether or not you categorize this as "questionable in nature".

3. Really, quite honestly, what section of the community is the eBay Community Watch Team watching over? Are they the equivalent of a crack-team of highly trained operatives, each skilled in their own personal talents? Is there a member who is smug, always lashing out at the world for some unknown reason or event that happened to him in the past? You know, like Batman?

Thanks in advance for taking the time to personally respond – you are the shining star in a dim country of Consumer Assistant Specialists. In fact, what kind of grades does one have to have in order to become a member of the "eBay Community Watch Team"? What would it take for me to get in on the auction-action!?

Look forward to hearing from you.

Best regards,

David Paulson

---

264 South Doheny Drive, #8 Beverly Hills, CA 90211

September 17, 2001

Gap, Inc.
One Harrison Street
San Francisco, CA 94105
Attn: Consumer Affairs

Dear Sir or Madam:

As an avid fan of the GAP brand, I usually make a special weekly trip to my local GAP location in the Beverly Center in Beverly Hills, California.

While there, I make a point to purchase at least something. This week, it was a pair of socks. Last week, a backpack. The week before, a pair of denim acid-washed jeans. And so on, and so on. You get the idea. This David Paulson is a GAP fanatic.

As an overly organized individual, I also have my walk-in closets divided into sections, and I am currently writing the various clothing companies I purchase a great deal of product from, in an attempt to request a picture of their President/CEO.

This picture, once received, will be framed in the highest quality metal-fiberglass black frame, covered in a plexiglass, protective coating, and hung above the area in my closet where I hang and store that particular company's product. So, on any given day, as I put on that GAP sweatshirt, I can shout out a friendly hello to the President/CEO who made my fashion sense possible.

A signed copy of your President/CEO would be extremely generous, but any type of picture will do. So far, I've already received signed pictures from the CEO's of Macy's, Marshall's, Ross' Dress-For-Less, and Foot Locker. I have also written a letter to Dateline NBC who may be interested in doing a short piece on my "Walk (In Closet) of Fame". Don't let your President/CEO be missing!!

Thanks a ton for you clothing, and your goodwill!

Minding the Gap,

David Paulson

---

264 South Doheny Drive, #8 Beverly Hills, CA 90211

December 10, 2001

David Paulson
264 South Doheny Drive #8
Beverly Hills, CA 90211

Dear Mr. Paulson:

Thank you for taking the time to write and express to us your
interest in a picture of our President/CEO. Unfortunately, we are
unable to furnish you with a picture. We apologize for any
inconvenience this may cause.

Again, thanks for thinking of us.

Sincerely,

Connie
Gap Customer Relations

August 31, 2001

The Quaker Oats Company
P.O. Box 049003
Chicago, IL 60604-9003

Dear Sir or Madam:

Let me just put milk to the bowl and say that I am a big fan of your Cap'n Crunch, Cap'n Crunch with Crunchberries, and Peanut Butter Cap'n Crunch cereals.

Unfortunately, I find that all three versions of your Cap'n Crunch line rip up the roof of my mouth, often leaving it raw and painfully uncomfortable for weeks after a breakfast meal with the Cap'n. I eat it with two-percent Milk and wondered if there was any way to make eating your cereal less painful?

My physician suggested possibly eating it with Soy Milk, but that stuff smells like crap. Any smart ideas?

All ripped up on the roof of my mouth,

David Paulson

264 South Doheny Drive, #8 Beverly Hills, CA 90211

September 12, 2001

Mr David Paulson
Apt 8
264 S Doheny Dr
Beverly Hills, CA 90211-2593

Dear Mr Paulson:

Thank you for taking the time to contact us. We're so sorry that you didn't enjoy Cap'n Crunch Cereal.

Our objective, pure and simple, is to make high-quality products that our consumers will choose again and again. We appreciate your input and will use your comments as we continuously work to improve our products.

We hope you enjoy trying one of our other products with the enclosed coupon.

Jennifer Higgins
Consumer Response Representative

Ref # 4200156A

www.quakeroats.com

87

December 10, 2001

Ms. Jennifer Higgins
Consumer Response Representative
The Quaker Oats Company
P.O. Box 049003
Chicago, IL 60604-9003

Dear Ms. Higgins:

I wasn't quite sure how to take your letter dated September 12, 2001 (REF# 4200156A), in which you seemingly tried to buy my silence (in regards to Cap'n Crunch ripping up the roof of my mouth) by shoving a four-dollar coupon in my face. In some countries, they call that "a bribe". In my country, I call that "a bribe".

Instead of shoving cold hard cash in my face, why not try and solve the problem instead? Why not ask those highly-paid "scientists" why it is that Cap'n Crunch rips up the roofs of people's mouths? I know it's not just me, either. I've secretly polled over 58 people in my current neighborhood who all agreed that eating Cap'n Crunch (even with milk) causes their gums to bleed, and results in a painful chewing experience for days after a breakfast meal.

I'd be happy to send back the four-dollar coupon in return for a thoughtful response that may provide a few solutions to this problem. Is it possible that Quaker Oats my want to create some kind of mouth-guard that consumers could wear while eating your product? I mean, hell, people wear night guards to protect their teeth from grinding in the wee hours of the night...why not provide mouth guards to protect against sharp Cap'n Crunch nuggets? I think it's a great idea.

Still...all ripped up on the roof of my mouth,

David Paulson

264 South Doheny Drive, #8 Beverly Hills, CA 90211

November 5, 2001

President & CEO
Cedar Point Amusement Park
1 Cedar Point Drive
Sandusky, Ohio 44870-5259

Dear Sir or Madam:

You can imagine my surprise, (as half a Ham & Cheese Hot Pocket hung from the corner of my mouth), as I watched a half-hour program on The Learning Channel that revealed the amazing fact that Cedar Point Amusement Park was "the largest of its kind in the entire country".

Almost immediately, I turned to my mini-toy poodle JACK TRICKS, revealing the same amazing piece of information. Ever since he was a little pup, little Jack Tricks has been a fan of all things related to speed. From sticking his head out the side window of my Ford Festiva, to riding the log flume at Disneyland, to running as fast as he can (head on) into the kitchen cabinets – little Jack Tricks has "a need for speed".

Although up until recently, we had planned on taking Jack to the local Magic Mountain amusement park here in Los Angeles…rumors had begun to swirl that the powers that be at Magic Mountain would not permit Jack on any of their rides. Including <u>Superman</u>. But Magic Mountain, as I've come to realize, is small peanuts. They're nothing like Cedar Point in it's grandiosity and customer service. That's why I'm writing you today.

I would like to arrange a trip to your amusement park and take Jack Tricks on what has been referred to as "the largest wood coaster in the World". I have fashioned a special harness that attaches him to my chest (much like a mother carries a baby), so that he will not fly out of the car while it's in motion, upside down, or hitting speeds in excess of 100 miles per hour. I just need your approval before I book the tickets to Ohio.

Thanks in advance for your consideration in this matter, and Jack says "hey".

Kindest regards,

David Paulson

---

264 South Doheny Drive, #8 Beverly Hills, CA 90211

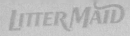

November 21, 2001

Mr. David Paulson
264 South Doheny Drive, #8
Beverly Hills, CA   90211

Dear Mr. Paulson:

Your letter to Cedar Point's president has been referred to me for review and response.

We are pleased you learned about Cedar Point through The Learning Channel and that you have an interest in visiting the park, in part, to afford Jack Tricks a ride on a few of our roller coasters.

Regrettably, we cannot grant approval to take your dog on our rides. Even though you may have fashioned a safety harness for him, we still must provide for the safe operation of the rides and the safety of all riders. We hope you understand this is an issue on which we cannot compromise.

Mr. Paulson, we are very proud of our park and sincerely hope you will be able to experience it someday. Thank you for contacting us.

Yours truly,

Richard J. Collingwood
Corporate Vice President
Administration

RJC/jmo

One Cedar Point Drive
Sandusky, Ohio
44870-5259
419.626.0830

October 2, 2001

Rubbermaid Home Products Division
ATTN: Consumer Services
1147 Akron Road
Wooster, Ohio 44691-6000

Dear Sir or Madam:

Believe it or not, those Myers kids are at it again. Last summer, they painted my RUBBERMAID garbage pails with such words as "STUPID CHEESE-HEAD", and "LOSER". In late August, they dumped ten pounds of turkey guts into them, causing them to smell up the entire block. And last week…they stole them.

The only problem is that I can't prove that Kyle and Ralphie Myers actually stole my RUBBERMAID cans. But, if I were to make an educated guess, I'd bet it was them. They're the kind of kids that grow up and kill their parents, if you know what I mean.

Anyway, I wondered if you could rush me two brand-new ROUGHNECK WHEELED GARBAGE CONTAINERS as soon as possible. I don't have my receipt from Target or anything, but I seem to remember that your company vows to replace any defective items. I'd appreciate it if you would ship them to the below address.

Using you, for my garbage!

David Paulson

264 South Doheny Drive, #8 Beverly Hills, CA 90211

Rubbermaid ®

Home Products

Oct 05, 2001

Mr. David Paulson
264 South Doheny Dr. #8
Beverly Hills, CA 90211

Dear Mr. Paulson

Thank you for your interest in Rubbermaid, and for taking the time to contact us regarding your product.

Although many of our products do not carry any type of written guarantee, we do stand behind the material and workmanship. Thus, if an item should fail under normal household use shortly after purchase due to faulty material or poor workmanship, we would forward a certificate to use to replace the item or reimburse in full.

I'm very sorry to hear of the trouble you have been having, but this particular incident does not fall under Rubbermaid warranty guidelines.

Thank you for using Rubbermaid products and for giving us the opportunity to address your concern.

Sincerely

Tara First
Consumer Services Department
Home Products Division

Rubbermaid Home Products
1147 Akron Road
Wooster, OH 44691
330.264.6464

www.rubbermaid.com

A **Newell Rubbermaid** Company.

December 10, 2001

Ms. Tara First
Consumer Services Department
Rubbermaid Home Products
1147 Akron Road
Wooster, Ohio 44691-6000

Dear Ms. First:

Thank you for <u>your</u> interest in <u>my</u> interest in Rubbermaid. I appreciated your letter dated October 5th, 2001.

I was glad to hear that your company stands behind your material and workmanship. I was also glad to hear that if an item (like my ROUGHNECK WHEELED GARBAGE CONTAINERS) should fail under household use, that you would forward a certificate to replace the item or reimburse in full.

I'd like to reiterate what happened to my Rubbermaid garbage cans now that we've confirmed the above information. My cans were destroyed under <u>normal</u> household usage, which just happened to be filling them with garbage, putting them outside my residence, and then finding them destroyed from the elements. In this case, the elements happened to be two pug-nosed, evil children named Kyle and Ralphie Myers.

I'm not sure you understand the emotional distress I'm under, constantly having to worry if these two demon-spawns are scratching hateful words on my cans, melting them with propane flames, or jumping on them in an attempt to, well, jump on them. For my neighborhood, this is <u>normal</u> household usage. And under your above statement, I believe this is a valid reason to reimburse me for my two cans.

If you disagree, please forward me the name and address of your superiors, or the name and home address of your company's President, so I may send the Myers children your way. Maybe then you'll re-examine your concept of what household usage really is.

Thank you so much,

David Paulson

---

264 South Doheny Drive, #8 Beverly Hills, CA 90211

December 11, 2001

Wendy's Customer Service
Wendy's International, Inc.
4288 W. Dublin-Granville Rd.
Dublin, OH 43017

Dear Sir or Madam:

People in this society are always telling you what you want to hear, and quite honestly I'm getting sick of it. I have been to over twenty-eight Wendy's locations in the continental United States and have asked at each location, "What's with the square burgers?"

Responses have ranged from, "Uh, that's just how they are", to "Our Manager isn't here right now, can you come back later?", to "That's how they come, frozen in a box." All valid answers, I guess, but not the truth.

I'm sure you're familiar with history, and how society used to think the world was flat. In reality, years later, people came to the realization that the world was, in fact, <u>round</u>! I'm wondering if, deep down, your corporation has stuck with the flat, square burgers because there's some connection to that historical anecdote, and the fact that your company wants to align itself with backwards thinking, days long gone, and the wrong side of the scientific world. I could be wrong, but that's why I'm writing.

So, once and for all, can we just lay this to rest? Why, in God's name, are your burgers square? Please, let me know before the holidays, as it's extremely important I know this information before New Year's Eve. Don't ask me why, just believe me when I tell you that this information will make the difference between a wonderful New Year's Eve and an evening in a dirty, scum-filled, alleyway.

Happy holidays,

David Paulson

264 South Doheny Drive, #8 Beverly Hills, CA 90211

Wendy's

OLD FASHIONED
HAMBURGERS.

December 20, 2001

Mr. David Paulson
264 South Doheny Dr. #8
Beverly Hills, CA 90211

Dear Mr. Paulson,

Thank you for taking the time to contact Wendy's Consumer Relations Department. At Wendy's, customer satisfaction is our number one priority, and we appreciate hearing our customers' opinions.

Wendy's has square hamburgers for two reasons. First, square hamburgers cover more of the bun so every bite you take has hamburger in it. Second, square hamburgers fit better on the rectangular grill in which they are cooked. This results in less wasted space and an evenly cooked, juicy hamburger. But our founder, Dave Thomas says we serve square hamburgers because, at Wendy's, we don't cut corners on quality!

We appreciate the time you took to send us your comments, Mr. Paulson . Please contact me again if we can be of service.

Sincerely,

Stacey Saunders
Consumer Relations
Wendy's International, Inc.

WENDY'S INTERNATIONAL, INC. / P.O. BOX 256 / 4288 WEST DUBLIN GRANVILLE ROAD, DUBLIN, OHIO 43017 / 614-764-3100

September 17, 2001

Sharp Electronics Corporation
Sharp Plaza
Mahwah, New Jersey 07430
Attn: Customer Service Department

Dear Sir or Madam:

Really, seriously... How close is too close to be standing in front of my Sharp Carousel Microwave Oven?

The only reason I ask is that I've been getting a lot of headaches lately, which happens to coincide with my purchasing a brand new microwave cook book, which has placed me right in front of my microwave from one to two hours a day.

If you could kindly respond with the proper distance I must be from my microwave when it's on, I'd really appreciate it.

Sincerely,

David Paulson

P.S. – The cookbook I recently bought, called "365 Ways to Microwave Chicken" is really quite wonderful if you like chicken. So if you do, like chicken, you may want to pick it up. Or possibly, even include it with your microwaves from here on out. Just an idea.

264 South Doheny Drive, #8 Beverly Hills, CA 90211

SHARP®

SHARP ELECTRONICS CORPORATION

Customer Assistance Center
1300 Naperville Dr.
Romeoville, IL 60441
(800) BE-SHARP

October 8, 2001

David Paulson
264 South Doheny Drive, #8
Beverly Hills, CA 90211

Refer to: Casefile 446396

Dear Mr. Paulson:

Thank you for writing to us regarding the safety aspects of your microwave oven. We sincerely hope that your fears are alleviated when you have finished reading this letter.

Please rest assured that there is no danger when you use your oven. The truth is the microwave oven is one of the safest appliances in your home. Manufacturers must meet strict radiation safety standards set by the government (Department of Health and Human Services) to ensure safety. Based on current knowledge about microwave ovens, when microwave ovens meet the rigorous requirements and are properly maintained, they are safe for home use. Underwriter Laboratories has set strict standards for the electrical aspects of microwave ovens. All Sharp ovens comply with all standards and in many instances are even stricter than the others.

The door seal on your microwave oven is designed to prevent any leakage of microwave energy from the oven, during cooking. The door seal does not need to be "air-tight" or "light-tight" in order to accomplish this function. Occasionally, moisture may appear around the oven door. You may also be able to see some small areas of light or feel warm air movement around the oven door. None of these situations is abnormal or necessarily indicated that your oven is leaking microwaves.

If you wish to have your oven checked for leakage, you may call our toll free number (800) BE-SHARP. Select option #1. Provide your zip code and you will be given the location of your nearest Sharp authorized service station.

Sincerely,

Customer Service Specialist
Customer Assistance Center

MICROWAVE MYTHS

Not everything you may have heard about microwave cooking is true. A number of myths persist because many people do not really understand how the microwave oven works. As you use your oven, you will discover that some of them are half-truths, while others are entirely false.

MYTH 1. Microwaves cook from the inside out. They certainly do not. Microwaves penetrate foods from the outside to a depth of about 1-inch. Small foods, fewer than 2 inches in diameter, are penetrated to the center from all sides. With larger foods, energy creates heat in the outer layer; then the heat moves to the center by conduction, as it does conventionally. A few foods may appear to cook more on the inside. One example is an egg. Energy penetrates to the center, where the fatty yolk becomes hotter than the white and cooks first.

MYTH 2. You can't use metal in a microwave oven. False. Metal reflects microwaves; the oven itself is made of metal so microwave energy cannot escape. Inside the oven, metal slows cooking because it keeps energy from reaching parts of the food. You can use the reflective properties of metal to protect foods, which might overcook in some areas. The magnetrons in most microwave ovens are designed so that they cannot be damaged by the use of metal in the oven.

MYTH 3. Dishes do not get hot in a microwave oven. Keep your potholders handy. A microwave-safe utensil will not be heated by microwave energy, but it will become hot from contact with hot food. Heat tends to equalize. A warm object heats the air around it, like a radiator in a cool room. When food becomes hot, some of this heat is transferred to the dish.

MYTH 4. Microwave foods do not stay hot. Not so. They cool at the same rate as conventionally heated foods and for the same reason. No matter how you heat foods, they cool faster if you serve them in a cool dish. One advantage of microwaving is that you can cook and serve in the same dish, so food stays hot longer.

MYTH 5. Foods do not brown in a microwave oven. True and false. Browning depends on fat content and the amount of cooking time in relation to food volume. Some foods do brown: such as bacon, roasts and turkey. Many small, moist foods cook so rapidly they do not have time to brown.

Pamela G. Rogel

December 10, 2001

Sharp Electronics Corporation
Customer Assistance Center
1300 Naperville Drive
Romeoville, IL 60441

Refer to: Casefile 446396

Dear Sir or Madam:

Thank you so much for your letter dated October 8th. Under normal circumstances, your letter might have alleviated my fears, except for the fact that my headaches have gotten worse ever since I wrote you my initial letter.

Mind you, I live in a neighborhood where people own those little yapping toy-dogs. You know, the kind that seem like some wild-eyed insane scientist grew them out of a petri dish just for fun, then pulled one over on America's dog-loving citizens and made a fortune selling them over the Internet? I mean, these things could double for rats in a really bad horror movie, if you know what I mean. But don't get me wrong, it's not the dogs creating my headaches.

I've even taken Tylenol, so when the headaches didn't go away, I was able to pretty much figure out that these aren't "normal" headaches. Normal headaches go away with Tylenol. Freaky-weird headaches do not. And I was further worried upon leaning my head inside the microwave oven – and feeling a burning sensation in my eyes.

Is there anything you can recommend that I do as a next step, in alleviating the pain I'm associating with my Sharp Microwave Oven? My doctor seems to think I should contact one of those people who handle microwave ovens that have hurt people, but I'd rather just ask you since you were so helpful in the past!

Micro-waving back atcha,

David Paulson

264 South Doheny Drive, #8 Beverly Hills, CA 90211

CIRCLE K FAN CLUB

December 12, 2001

Circle K
Customer Service
P.O. Box 52085 (DC 73)
Phoenix, AZ 85072-2085

Dear Sir or Madam:

Ever since Keanu Reeves uttered the phrase, "Something strange is afoot at the Circle K" in the movie Bill & Ted's Excellent Adventure, clubs like ours have been meeting on a bi-monthly basis to celebrate all that is CIRCLE K.

As a result of our upcoming "CIRCLE K PARTY-ON WEEKEND EXTRAVAGANZA", I am writing to request a satin or cotton flag with the CIRCLE K logo on it. This flag will fly at full mast during the entire weekend, saluting your company and all it does to support the "Something strange is afoot at the Circle K" values and mentality.

Please let me know if there is any cost for the flag, although I believe it should be complimentary as we are saluting you as opposed to CIRCLE K saluting its own Fan Club. Although, if you were saluting your own fan club, you'd probably want to give that flag to them for free, too, so it really all makes sense in the end if you think about it.

Best regards,

David Paulson
Co-Founder, Circle K Fan Club

264 South Doheny Drive, #8 Beverly Hills, CA 90211

PHILLIPS 66 COMPANY
West Coast Region
495 E. Rincon #150, Corona, Ca 92879

December 20, 2001

David Paulson
264 South Doheny Dr. #8
Beverly Hills, Ca. 90211

Dear David;

I am writing in response to your request for a Circle K flag for your Circle K Fan Club. We currently do not have such a flag pre-printed. I am in the process of seeing about getting one printed for you. If you would give me a call and let me know when your "Circle K Party-On Weekend Extravaganza" will be taking place, I will try to accommodate your request.

Regards,

West Coast Region Admin. Asst.
Phillips 66 Retail Marketing

CIRCLE K FAN CLUB

December 21, 2001

West Coast Region Admin. Asst.
C/o Phillips 66 Company (a.k.a. Circle K)
West Coast Region
495 E. Rincon #150
Corona, CA 92879

Dear Friendly West Coast Region Admin Asst:

Just when you think the world is coming to its end and that there's really no hope left whatsoever – you get a letter like the one I received from you today regarding the "CIRCLE K PARTY-ON WEEKEND EXTRAVAGANZA"!

If you must know, James Bilhorn, our Vice-President in charge of philanthropy was giving me a lot of crap lately because he didn't feel as though I had the flag situation under control. He even went so far as to bring up a motion in our last "Party-On Meeting" to have me replaced with someone who had a better handle on flags and how to get them. As I'm sure you can imagine, I called him as soon as I got your letter. Needless to say, he was pretty quiet on the other end of the phone. His plans at impeaching one of the Co-Founders of the Circle K Fan Club would not come to fruition! So thanks, for that.

I tried calling you as soon as I slammed the phone down on Bilhorn, but for some reason it doesn't seem to be going through. I'm not sure if I am supposed to dial a one before your area code or what – the damn phone company has added all these codes you have to dial now with stars and asterixes and for the life of me I couldn't quite figure it out. Frustration grew to anger, then I sat down and decided to just contact you the old fashioned way. So here I am.

To answer your question, the "CIRLCE K PARTY-ON WEEKEND EXTRAVAGANZA" will be taking place during the weekend of January 25-27th, 2002 in Torrance, California. We have secured a great little rest-area off the 405 freeway where we believe local hooligans will not pose a problem. I don't know if you've heard, but Torrance has become overrun with these hooligans, intent on stealing citizens' oversized Football jerseys, Palm Pilots (if they have them), and expensive sneakers. What about money, you ask? Yeah, they take that too.

Let me know when you think the Circle K flag will arrive so I may call Bilhorn again and rub it in his face. He deserves it, you know. He's had it in for me from the start and it's nice to know the guy's finally going to have to eat some dirt. For real.

Party on,

David Paulson
Co-Founder, Circle K Fan Club

264 South Doheny Drive, #8 Beverly Hills, CA 90211

PHILLIPS 66 COMPANY
West Coast Region
495 E. Rincon #150, Corona, Ca 92879

January 9, 2002

David Paulson
264 South Doheny Dr. #8
Beverly Hills, Ca. 90211

Dear David;

Enclosed you will find the Circle K flag as you requested. Please note this flag has been "special ordered" for you and is the <u>only one</u> in existence. I hope your Circle K Fan Club enjoys the flag, and that your "Circle K Party-On Weekend Extravaganza" goes off without a hitch! Maybe you could send some photos of your event. I look forward to hearing from you.

Regards,

West Coast Region Admin. Asst.
Phillips 66 Retail Marketing

CIRCLE K FAN CLUB

January 11, 2002

West Coast Region Admin. Asst.
C/o Phillips 66 Company (a.k.a. Circle K)
West Coast Region
495 E. Rincon #150
Corona, CA 92879

Dear Extremely Generous West Coast Region Admin. Asst:

You are like the Moses of Corporate America! Having parted the seas of complication and afflicted one James Bilhorn with the equivalent of locusts as a result of one selfless act. That act just-happened to be the provision of this brand-new Circle K flag! (Actually, that makes you more like God than Moses since you "handed down" the flag to me, but let's not get crazy over semantics here.)

I wanted to provide you with a detailed schedule of the event in case you happen to be in the neighborhood during the weekend of January 25-27th, 2002. It is as follows:

Friday, January 25th

6:00-7PM:	Check in/Buffet Style Dinner Provided By "Marshmallow Fluff"
7:00-8PM:	Inspirational Speech by David Paulson: "Why We Must Party-On"
8:00-10PM:	Screening of "*Bill & Ted's Excellent Adventure*"

Saturday, January 26th

10:00-NOON:	Brunch Provided By "Sir Speedy's Beef & Bread Products"
NOON-1PM:	Team Up and Compete In The "Surf While Bloated" Relay Race
1:00-2PM:	Siesta (a.k.a. Rest From Being Bloated), Followed by Sack Lunch
2:00-4PM:	Screening of "*Bill & Ted's Bogus Journey*"
4:00-6PM:	Inspirational Speech by James Bilhorn: "Partying On in 2002: The Realities and Drawbacks"
6:00-7PM:	BBQ "See If You Can Find The Hot Dog" Dinner Provided by "Highlights Magazine"
7:00-9PM:	Screening of "*Behind the Scenes: Bill & Ted's Bogus Journey*"
9:00-11PM:	Screening of "*Bill & Ted's Excellent Adventure*"
11:00-1AM:	Screening of Keanu Reeve's Selected Scenes from "Dangerous Liaisons"

Sunday, January 27th

9:00-10AM:	Breakfast Provided By "Denny's"
10:00-11AM:	Checkout/Sign Guestbook/Purchase "Party On Mantra Magazine"
NOON-2PM:	Encore Presentation (If Necessary) of "*Bill & Ted's Excellent Adventure*"

264 South Doheny Drive, #8 Beverly Hills, CA 90211

And while all the above events are going on, my friendly neighborhood administrative assistant, the flag that you generously provided will be whipping in the wind, inspiring all to live the mantra that "Something Strange Is Afoot At The Circle K"!   And all thanks to you! Hats off!

Party on,

David Paulson
Co-Founder, Circle K Fan Club

P.S. – I know it's a strange request, but could we get a picture of you to include in our "Party-On Weekend Extravaganza" information booklet? You know, just as a way to thank you and show people who was responsible for the flag?

September 6, 2001

Yahoo! Inc.
701 First Avenue
Sunnyvale, California 94089
Attn: Customer Service Representative

Dear Sir or Madam:

Let's face it. Sometimes, companies hire other companies to create engaging radio advertisements that they hope will increase their client base. And sometimes, they fail miserably, and offend a great portion of the public in the process. Welcome to the latter, Yahoo, Incorporated.

I recently heard a radio spot for your website that appears to make fun of honest, middle American folks like myself. As a native of South Carolina, I can honestly say that I am indeed one of those people who yodel and sing songs with my cousins on the back porch. And here comes Yahoo, seeking to make fun of just that pastime.

Your recent radio spot is the equivalent of using the "n" word for African Americans, or the "p" word for those of Middle-Eastern backgrounds. Your commercial is basically saying that I'm stupid, and too idiotic to even learn how to use the Web Wide Net.

Recently, while visiting my hometown for a sad occasion (a funeral if you must know), your radio spot was a big part of everyone's conversations. And you should know, there's a group of people out there, growing fast, who don't appreciate the way you treat the Middle-American citizens who go to your DSL site every so often.

I'd appreciate it if you'd stop airing the commercial on the local radio stations here in Los Angeles, as well as the ones back in South Carolina. As for the other states, I don't know if they're airing there since my radio doesn't reach that far.

Thank you,

David Paulson

264 South Doheny Drive, #8 Beverly Hills, CA 90211

YAHOO!™

September 10, 2001

Dear Mr. Paulson,

Thank you for your letter of 6-Sep-01 concerning Yahoo!'s radio advertisements.

I appreciate your taking the time to write to us, and I will make sure that copies of your letter go to the appropriate Yahoo! team members for their review.

Thank you,

Yahoo! Customer Care

December 12, 2001

Starbucks Customer Relations
P.O. Box 3717
Seattle, WA 98124-3717

Dear Sir or Madam:

Well, congratulations! You did it. According to your "Year 2000 Fiscal Report", your company has over 3,500 locations world-wide, serving more than 12 million customers per week. And you current goal to have more than 20,000 locations, is now "well within your reach". Apparently, the conspiracy theories about your company seeking "world domination" are more than conspiracy theories.

My question is simply, where will it all end? At what point with the leaders of your company decide that enough is enough? A Starbucks in every city, on every corner, perhaps in every apartment complex throughout the World? On the moon? I mean, c'mon, there is such a thing as overdoing it, don't you think?

I personally don't drink coffee. Never have, never will. But for me, it's a personal reason, stemming from a strange incident in a cotton-field that befell me in my early teens. Because of my refusals to imbibe your product my life is safe from any meddling that Starbucks seeks to inflict upon me. But what of the helpless ones? Those who cannot fight back against your soy-milk drenched lies?

Aaah, but what is the real truth? Why is Starbucks so hell bent on conquest? Why do they grow each year like an infection that cannot be stopped? This, is the question I would like the answer to. Sooner than later, please.

Holiday wishes to you and yours,

David Paulson

---

264 South Doheny Drive, #8 Beverly Hills, CA 90211

Starbucks Coffee Company
PO Box 34067
Seattle, WA 98124-1067
206/447-1575

December 19, 2001

David Paulson
264 Doheny Drive #8
Beverly Hills, CA 90211

Dear Mr. Paulson,

Thank you for contacting Starbucks Coffee Company. I was disappointed to hear that you do not want Starbucks to continue growing.

Starbucks goal is to provide customers with the world's finest coffee in a friendly environment and convenient neighborhood locations. Starbucks prides itself on being good citizens locally and globally by giving back to its communities in many ways.

The stores employ local people and serve pastries made by local bakeries. In addition, Starbucks contributes to food banks and sponsors community programs that support children, the arts, the environment, and AIDS research. For example, Starbucks stores consistently donate coffee beans that are more than seven days old, as well as any left-over pastries to its local food banks. Also, many of our store managers are actively involved with their local Chamber of Commerce.

I hope this letter adequately demonstrates Starbucks aim as a company. If you have any further questions, I invite you to call the Customer Relations department at 1-800-23-LATTE.

Warm Regards,

Casey

Casey E.
Customer relations representative

December 27, 2001

Starbucks Customer Relations
P.O. Box 3717
Seattle, WA 98124-3717
Attn: Casey E.

Dear Casey:

Thank you for your letter dated December 19, 2001. Although I understand your attempt was to try and alleviate my fears that Starbucks is nothing more than an evil conglomerate seeking to take over the Earth, you did something even worse. Your examples of Starbucks' activities of goodwill appear to be nothing more than cruel jokes on the less-fortunate.

You mention that Starbucks consistently donates coffee beans that are more than seven days old along with left-over pastries to food banks. Now, I don't know if you've tasted pastries just <u>one</u> <u>day</u> <u>old</u> at Starbucks, but they're hard, stale, and un-tasty. And old coffee beans? Are these examples selfless, or <u>selfish</u>?

And to simply throw in the afterthought that some store managers are involved with their local Chamber of Commerce! The nerve! As an active member of my local Chamber of Commerce, and the person who spearheaded our recent "Sister City Celebration" (in which citizens of Beverly Hills and Cannes, France eat strange and eclectic foods to show people how accepting we are of foreigners), I can tell you that no manager of a Starbucks was ever involved in our planning! Bet you didn't think you'd get caught in <u>that</u> lie! Well, you did, smart-guy.

I think it's time for you to be honest about what's really going on, Casey. Instead of simply repeating and copying text from some Starbucks manifesto, maybe you can shed some light on why Starbucks is really expanding at such an alarming rate. I promise, I won't share the info with anyone.

Happy new year,

David Paulson

264 South Doheny Drive, #8 Beverly Hills, CA 90211

October 3, 2001

Humane Society of the United States
2100 L Street, NW
Washington, DC 20037
Attn: Contributions

Dear Sir or Madam:

I love animals. More than most of your current employees probably do. I'm the kind of guy who goes out in the street, armed with a bag of milk bones and cans of tuna fish, and feed the animals that walk the streets of Los Angeles. To some people, I'm like a superhero of sorts, or the Robin Hood of the animal kingdom. But I want to give more.

Unfortunately, I don't have the financial stability to donate a large amount of cash, but I do have something else that's much more valuable than that. I call it... "heart". And along with that "heart" comes a spacious one-bedroom apartment, here in the "heart" of Beverly Hills. My apartment has a bathroom, a kitchen, a bunch of great carpet, and a bedroom with lots of pillows and such. I would like to offer up my apartment as a haven for stray animals.

I have tried, on my own, to corral animals into my apartment, but for some reason they often run away back into the streets. And I can't keep my door shut all the time, because you can imagine the smell that gets stuck inside. But I figured, since the Humane Society is the equivalent of the President of the Animal Kingdom, any animal you manually place into my apartment, will have to stay here.

Let me know what type of preparations I must make in order to make my apartment, animal-haven ready. I vacuum regularly, so there isn't much dust!

A friend to animals everywhere,

David Paulson

264 South Doheny Drive, #8 Beverly Hills, CA 90211

THE HUMANE SOCIETY
OF THE UNITED STATES™

October 17, 2001

Dear Mr. Paulson:

Thank you for contacting The Humane Society of the United States (HSUS) regarding being a foster parent for homeless animals. We think it is great that you want to open your heart and home to help animals in need.

As you may know, fostering is generally the placement of special-case animals into temporary homes until they are suitable for adoption. This may mean animals that are too young, sick or under socialized for adoption. Some rescue groups do not have a shelter and use foster parents to house all of their animals for adoption.

First, I should tell you that we do not shelter animals here at The Humane Society of the United States (HSUS). Instead, we work for animals on the national level, through public education projects, by investigating large-scale animal abuses, by working for humane laws, and through the court system. The HSUS is not a parent organization for local humane societies, animal shelters, or animal care and control agencies. We are in contact with local groups regularly, however, and share with them our guidelines for operating shelters, along with a wealth of other publications.

You will need to contact your local humane society or rescue group to see if they have a foster program. To find your local shelter check the Yellow Pages of your Phone Book under "animal shelter," "humane society," or "animal control." You can also call Information.

Depending on the organization's program, you can expect to fill out a volunteer application or foster care agreement and be required to attend an orientation session. Before you agree to be a foster parent, ask the organization about its adoption policies, what its goals for the foster program are, what costs will be involved and what you will be responsible for, and if they provide care information for sick, injured, young and under socialized animals.

It takes a special person to be a foster parent. Fostering requires a great deal of time and commitment and the type of person who can take home a needy animal to care for, bond with, and then return to the shelter. This is not easy, but the joy and satisfaction that fostering provides is extremely rewarding.

Thank you again for contacting us. Please let us know if we can be of assistance to you in the future.

Sincerely,

Krista Fowler
Outreach Assistant
Companion Animals and Equine Protection

Promoting the protection of all animals
2100 L Street, NW, Washington, DC 20037 ▪ 202-452-1100 ▪ Fax: 202-778-6132 ▪ www.hsus.org

September 17, 2001

Pentel of America, Ltd.
2805 Columbia Street
Torrance, CA 90509
Attn: Customer Service Dept.

Dear Sir or Madam:

I recently found myself in front of the television, doing the crossword puzzle as I often do on Sunday nights. In fact, I find that it's a welcomed diversion from the week prior – filled with bossy supervisors forcing me to do things that quite honestly, I find to be degrading and disgusting.

Nevertheless, I was using your Pentel Rolling Writer to complete the latest People Magazine Crossword Puzzle when I came across a confusing entry that posed the question, "23 Across' Partner in Crime". Truly, it stumped me, and I started to gnaw on the back of your Pentel product in an attempt to spark my brain.

Instead, my teeth punctured the back of your product, sending waves upon waves of salty-tasting ink into my mouth. I was up immediately, spitting out as much as I could, but my nighttime mouth guard (I grind my teeth constantly) was stained beyond all recognition.

I wondered if there was any way to wash out the ink from my mouth-guard, and if I was under any permanent danger having swallowed about half of your Pentel's ink capacity?

Write back soon!

David Paulson

264 South Doheny Drive, #8 Beverly Hills, CA 90211

PENTEL OF AMERICA, LTD.
2805 Columbia Street
Torrance, California 90509
Phone (310) 320-3831

October 3, 2001

Mr. David Paulson
264 South Doheny Drive #8
Beverly Hills, CA 90211

Dear Mr. Paulson:

Thank you for your letter regarding your Pentel pen. We regret any inconvenience you have experienced.

We wish to assure you that the ink in the Rolling Writer is non-toxic. We are enclosing a Material Data Safety Sheet for your review.

The ink is water-based; however, we do not have any particular advice as to removing it from your mouth guard.

If you should have any further questions, please contact us at (800) 262-1127.

Thank you.

Sincerely,
Pentel of America, Ltd.

Material Safety Data Sheet

May be used to comply with
OSHA's Hazard Communication Standard,
29 CFR 1910.1200. Standard must be
consulted for specific requirements.

U.S. Department of Labor

Occupational Safety and Health Administration
(Non-Mandatory Form)
Form Approved
OMB No. 1218-0072

IDENTITY (As Used on Label and List)	Note: Blank spaces are not permitted. If any item is not applicable, or no information is available, the space must be marked to indicate that.
R100 Rolling Writer (Roller Pen)	

Section I

Manufacturer's Name	Emergency Telephone Number
Pentel of America, Ltd.	(800) 421-1419
Address (Number, Street, City, State, and ZIP Code)	Telephone Number for Information
2715 Columbia Street	(310) 320-3831
Torrance, CA 90503	**Date Prepared** 3/8/93
	Signature of Preparer (optional) Quality Assurance Department

Section II — Hazardous Ingredients/Identity Information

Hazardous Components (Specific Chemical Identity; Common Name(s))	OSHA PEL	ACGIH TLV	Other Limits Recommended	% (optional)
Ethylene glycol	N/A	N/A	N/A	10%

Section III — Physical/Chemical Characteristics

Boiling Point	386.6	Specific Gravity (H₂O = 1)	N/A
Vapor Pressure (mm Hg.)	N/A	Melting Point	N/A
Vapor Density (AIR = 1)	N/A	Evaporation Rate (Butyl Acetate = 1)	N/A
Solubility in Water	Miscible		
Appearance and Odor	N/A		

Section IV — Fire and Explosion Hazard Data

Flash Point (Method Used)	240°F	Flammable Limits	N/A	LEL N/A	UEL N/A
Extinguishing Media	N/A				
Special Fire Fighting Procedures	N/A				
Unusual Fire and Explosion Hazards	N/A				

(Reproduce locally)

OSHA 174, Sept. 1985

September 17, 2001

Six Flags Theme Parks, Inc.
400 Interpace Parkway Building C, 3rd Floor
Parsippany, NJ 07054
Attn: Six Flags Magic Mountain Consumer Relations

Dear Sir or Madam:

As a resident of Los Angeles, I have heard many things about Six Flag's Magic Mountain, including the fact that it's currently overrun by gangs and that any visit to your park during the nighttime hours will most likely result in a mugging or violent scuffle.

I'm not quite sure who it was that said it, but I keep hearing it all over the place and wanted to find out if it was true.

Sincerely,

David Paulson

P.S. – Do you guys serve "churros" at Magic Mountain? Because I once took a psychology class at a local junior college where I was taught that food items such as that, (with such a high quotient of sugar) actually causes individuals to act erratic and brings out subdued violent tendencies. So, if you do, and the above is true – simply removing "churros" from your food items may change a lot of things.

264 South Doheny Drive, #8 Beverly Hills, CA 90211

26101 Magic Mountain Parkway

Valencia, California 91355

Phone (661) 255-4100

www.sixflags.com

October 18, 2001

Mr. David Paulson
264 South Doheny Drive, #8
Beverly Hills, CA 90211

Dear Mr. Paulson:

Thank you for writing us in regards to the comments you heard about Six Flags Magic Mountain.

As a family theme park hosting millions of guests every year, our top priority is to provide the best quality entertainment possible. We regret that you may have heard inaccurate information about our park. Over the past 30 years, Six Flags Magic Mountain has been dedicated to providing a safe and fun family experience for all.

The safety and security of our guests and employees has, and always will be, our number one priority. We have a zero tolerance policy for misbehavior and our guests know it. In the rare case of guest misbehavior, our security teams are trained to deal effectively with any situation.

You can be assured that a visit to Six Flags Magic Mountain is an enjoyable experience and we will continue to provide a very safe environment at all times.

Again, thank you for your time and your comments. We value you as a Guest and look forward to seeing you in the park soon.

Sincerely,

Andy Gallardo
Public Relations Manager
Six Flags Magic Mountain

December 11, 2001

Public Relations Dept.
Six Flags Theme Parks, Inc.
400 Interpace Parkway Building C, 3rd Floor
Parsippany, NJ 07054

Dear Sir or Madam:

Thank you for your letter dated October 18th, in which you informed me that "over the past 30 years, Six Flags Magic Mountain has been dedicated to providing a safe and fun family experience for all." Assuming that is true, see if you can guess which safe and fun experiences I had on my last trip to your park:

===

Question #1: Did the man who accosted you at the urinal in the Magic Mountain bathroom threaten you with…

[a] A gun
[b] A bat
[c] A sharpened blade made from toothpicks
[d] A churro

Question #2: Was your car "keyed" in the Magic Mountain parking lot by…

[a] Hoodlums
[b] Hoodlums disguised as park staff
[c] Park staff who are generally just hoodlums
[d] Your grandmother

===

I think you get my point. Why not forward me a list of these "fun experiences" that you've been standing behind, Mr. Gallardo. Let's put water to weight. Let's get the ink out of the puddle-jumper. Let's just, for once, answer a question that has been asked of you.

Sincerely,

David Paulson

264 South Doheny Drive, #8 Beverly Hills, CA 90211

September 24, 2001

McCormick & Company
211 Schilling Circle
Hunt Valley, MD 21031
Attn: Customer Service Deptartment

Dear Sir or Madam:

My friend Dale told me that pepper actually stains your colon, and since the last thing I
want is a black-stained colon, I figured I'd ask and make sure he wasn't pulling my leg.

Best regards,

David Paulson

P.S. – If the above is really true, you may want to initiate some spin control on the subject,
because you know how crazy people got over cigarettes turning people's lungs black!
I'd hate to see the same thing happen to a company like yours.

---

264 South Doheny Drive, #8 Beverly Hills, CA 90211

McCORMICK & COMPANY, INC. 211 SCHILLING CIRCLE, HUNT VALLEY, MD 21031-1100, USA, (410) 527-6000 FAX (410) 527-6267

**McCORMICK/SCHILLING
DIVISION**

September 28, 2001

Mr. David Paulson
264 S Doheny Dr Apt 8
Beverly Hills, CA 90211-2593

Dear Mr. Paulson:

Thank you for taking the time to contact us. We appreciate your interest in our Black Pepper and welcome the opportunity to be of assistance to you.

McCormick & Co., Inc. only responds to spice and cooking questions. Any medical concerns should be directed to your physician.

Please accept the enclosed with our compliments. If we can be of further assistance, please call us at 1-800-632-5847, Monday through Friday, 9:30AM to 5PM Eastern Time. We hope to have the continued pleasure of serving you.

Sincerely,

Consumer Affairs Specialist

Enclosures

Ref # 208276

October 7, 2001

Consumer Affairs Specialist
McCormick & Company
211 Schilling Circle
Hunt Valley, MD 21031

Dear Sir or Madam:

I was quite taken aback by your recent letter, in which you informed me that McCormick & Company only responds to spice and cooking questions, and will not address any medical concerns in regards to your products!! I couldn't believe it!

Am I to take that to mean, if I collapse on the floor of my kitchen, having inhaled a large amount of your Black Pepper, that you'd prefer I call my physician instead of contacting you? Is that supposed to mean that, if I'm wondering about the side-effects caused by consuming some of your spices, that my physician should know more about the safety of your products than your corporation? It seems awfully strange to me.

I did call my physician, however, upon your request. His response, about whether or not your company's Black Pepper will stain my colon was that he "had no idea" and that the manufacturer should know whether this was true or not. He suggested I write your company a letter. And again, here I am.

And so I ask you, please, can you tell me whether or not your company knows if your Black Pepper turns people's colons black? I'm sure McCormick & Company did some testing on laboratory rats at some point, somewhere!

Best regards,

David Paulson

P.S. – Since you seem so intent on answering cooking questions, can you please tell me whether or not you think that McCormick & Company's Black Pepper would go good in a vegetable lasagna dish?

August 28, 2001

Procter & Gamble
PO BOX 599
Cincinnati, OH 45201

Dear Sir or Madam:

As a proponent of clean and healthy teeth, I sometimes use CREST four or five times throughout the day in brushing away food particles and plaque.

Recently, when I had some time on my hands, I got around to reading the back of your CREST "Neat Squeeze" bottle and came across some very alarming text that read, "WARNING: If you accidentally swallow more than used for brushing, seek professional help or contact a poison control center immediately."

Often times, after brushing, there's a little bit of toothpaste left in my mouth, and instead of just spitting it out into the sink, I sometimes swallow it. It's refreshing, what can I say. But if my calculations are correct, over the last ten or so years, I've swallowed about the equivalent of eight and a half bottles of CREST. Needless to say, your warning caused me great concern.

Why should people contact a poison control center? What does swallowing an excessive amount of CREST do to the human body? As your "Neat Squeeze" bottle does not include any of the health issues caused by swallowing excessive amounts of CREST, my imagination got the better of me until finally I had to sit down and write you a letter.

Please respond to this letter and let me know if I've done unthinkable damage to my body. And if so, what steps can I take to reverse the damage?

Sincerely,

David Paulson

264 South Doheny Drive, #8 Beverly Hills, CA 90211

Procter&Gamble

Public Affairs Division
P.O. Box 599, Cincinnati, Ohio 45201-0599
www.pg.com

Our ref: 2802550
September 20, 2001

MR DAVID PAULSON
264 SOUTH DOHENY DR #8
BEVERLY HILLS CA 90211

Dear Mr. Paulson:

Thanks for contacting P&G about Crest. There is no safety risk to an adult or child who may occasionally swallow a small amount of toothpaste while brushing. The product label cautions consumers not to swallow the product because ingestion of a large amount of toothpaste would be expected to cause nausea, vomiting or diarrhea. This is because certain ingredients that are common in toothpastes have the potential to cause stomach irritation if enough is ingested. We would simply recommend that you spit out the toothpaste after brushing your teeth rather than swallowing it.

In 1996, the FDA required new wording for toothpaste packages containing fluoride. The FDA did not intend for the warning information to scare people or imply toothpaste is no longer a safe product to use. This information is required for all fluoride toothpaste products, not just Crest. The purpose is to let people know who to call for help and determine if the situation needs further medical attention.

Sincerely,

Consumer Relations - CCT

For Office Use Only:
1 CO 009170
1 OE 009001

EXPIRES 09/30/2002

28163

Crest

$1.00 Off One Any

537000610767   81000281632

RETAILER: AUTHENTICITY TEST PRINTED ON BACK OF THIS COUPON
PROCTER & GAMBLE® NAME IS REPEATED IN SMALL BLUE TYPE

DAVID PAULSON
2802550

September 21, 2001

President
Procter & Gamble
1 Procter & Gamble Plz.
Cincinnati, OH 45202

Dear Sir or Madam:

As I often read while taking a bathroom pit stop, I recently found myself looking at the text on the back of one of your CHARMIN packages. Quite honestly, it so confused me, I couldn't finish doing my business. If you know what I mean.

There's a chart on the back of your package that says CHARMIN is soft, strong, and thick. At the same time, it says that CHARMIN ULTRA is softer, stronger, and thicker. On top of that, it tells me that CHARMIN PLUS has Aloe. I know the United States is a country of democracy and choices, but this is ridiculous!!

Why would I purchase CHARMIN now that I know that CHARMIN ULTRA is better in every single way? And why would I purchase CHARMIN ULTRA if I knew that CHARMIN PLUS has Aloe? And since I'm one of those white, pasty guys, and I'm always getting burnt by the sun, if I can get a product with Aloe, you bet your bottom I'm going to!

What's your thought-process here? Why so much confusion? Why not just make it easy for everyone and make one CHARMIN product that includes all the best elements?

Just so you know, I called your 1-800 number to ask this question, and was met with confusion as well. Your operators eventually told me to "just buy whichever one you want, we've got other calls to take care of". I thought it was a little insensitive, especially since we're talking about my quest for a "quality-wiping experience".

Can someone please clear this all up? Until you do, I'm going to have a really hard time deciding in which way to wipe my butt.

Sincere, Sincerely, and Ultra Sincerely!

David Paulson

---

264 South Doheny Drive, #8 Beverly Hills, CA 90211

P&G
External
Relations

The Procter & Gamble Company
General Offices
1 P&G Plaza
Cincinnati, Ohio 45202-3315
www.pg.com

Our ref: 3030037
October 25, 2001

MR DAVID PAULSON
264 SOUTH DHENY DRIVE #8
BEVERLY HILLS CA 90211

Dear Mr. Paulson:

Thanks for contacting us with your creative suggestions for Charmin.

We appreciate your loyalty and are glad you let us know of your interest in another
version of Charmin. Making products people want and like is what we're all about. I'm
sharing your feedback with the rest of our Charmin Team.

Please bear in mind that we try to satisfy the diverse wants of the public. "To each his
own" as they
say.

Thanks again for getting in touch with us.

Sincerely,

Consumer Relations - PT

For Office Use Only:
1 CO 009220
1 OE 009001

EXPIRES 09/30/2002

PLEASE WRITE IN RETAIL PRICE

28609

FREE PRODUCT

Charmin

One 4, 6, 9 or 12 Roll Pack Any Version

RETAILER: AUTHENTICITY TEST PRINTED ON BACK OF THIS COUPON
PROCTER & GAMBLE'S NAME IS REPEATED IN SMALL BLUE TYPE

5270004410019

81000286093

DAVID PAULSON
3030037

December 13, 2001

Nyquil
c/o Procter & Gamble
1 P&G Plaza
Cincinnatti OH 45202
Attn: Nyquil Brand Manager

Dear Sir or Madam:

After working forty-hours a week in an office where people simply don't cover their mouths, I've been privy to hundreds of spores of infected diseases on a weekly basis. Finally, this past month, it caught up with me.

Sickly, pale, and quite honestly surprised at the amount of milky-white substance dripping from a few of my orifices, I went to the store to pick up my favorite "nighttime, sniffling, sneezing, coughing, aching, stuffy-head, fever, so you can rest medicine"! I went home immediately and took the directed dosage. I woke up three days later.

I'm not kidding you. In the three days that passed, I was dead to the world. Stirred not by telephone, doorbell, earthquake, and my roommate screaming and pushing me with all his might. I was, for all intensive purposes, a modern day Rip Van Winkle.

It got me to thinking, and made me a tad nervous. Is Nyquil supposed to put you out for that long without any kind of consciousness whatsoever? I, personally, find it dangerous. Especially if there had been a fire or tidal wave that had engulfed my residence during my "suspended animation". Can you or your doctors over there at One P&G Plaza tell me what you think happened? Should I see my physician about this?

Kindest regards,

David Paulson

264 South Doheny Drive, #8 Beverly Hills, CA 90211

Procter&Gamble

The Procter & Gamble Distributing Company
Health Care Research Center
8700 Mason-Montgomery Road
Mason, Ohio 45040-9462

January 7, 2002

Mr. David Paulston
264 south Doheny #8
Beverly Hills, CA 90211

Dear Mr. Paulston:

Thank you for contacting us about the symptoms you experienced that coincided with your use of NyQuil®. By way of introduction, I am a representative of the Medical Affairs Division of The Procter & Gamble Distributing Company. Our department is charged with the responsibility of reviewing all reports involving our product's safety. I am sorry you had a problem and appreciate that you brought this matter to my attention.

Please let me assure you that before we introduce any of our products to the marketplace, they undergo a battery of tests to assure their safety and effectiveness. In accordance with company standards, Procter & Gamble has been monitoring the safety and use of NyQuil since the product was first acquired. Our company strives to manufacture and package all of our products with a strong emphasis for quality. All of the ingredients in NyQuil are Food and Drug Administration authorized materials that have been extensively tested for human safety.

We would not expect the symptoms reported to Consumer Relations to be related to the use of NyQuil, however, we cannot determine the cause of your symptoms. We recommend you discontinue use of NyQuil. You may wish to consult your physician or health care practitioner regarding your symptoms. They are the best source of information about your medical history and health. After discussing this situation with your physician or health care practitioner further, if he/she needs more information regarding this product, please have him/her call us at our Professional Relations toll-free telephone number at 1-800-358-8707.

Again, I am sorry you had a problem and thank you for taking the time to contact us. The information you provided will be included in the safety records of this product.

Sincerely,

OTC Medical Affairs Division
The Procter & Gamble Distributing Co.
PER # CIO02000115

August 31, 2001

Mr. William Wrigley Jr.
Wm. Wrigley Jr. Company
Wrigley Building
410 North Michigan Avenue
Chicago, Illinois   USA

Dear Mr. Wrigley, Jr.:

With today's technological advances, how is it that the flavor of your JUICYFRUIT gum lasts about one minute per stick?

I have chewed other brands of gum, and each one surpasses yours by providing flavor and enjoyment past ten minutes of chewing time. But JUICYFRUIT continually falls short of such time.

However, I love the flavor of your gum, and so that is why I'm writing with these questions. I figure, if there was a way to make the flavor of one stick of JUICYFRUIT last a few minutes longer, you'd keep people from referring to JUICYFRUIT as "that old gum from the fifties". Trust me, I listen…people say that.

Have you ever chewed Trident's Cinnamon gum? Chew that for an hour, then stick your tongue in the center of it and we'll see how long you can keep it there. It stings, bad!

Sincerely,

David Paulson

P.S. – My Uncle Bob tells me that the reason the flavor disappears so quickly is so that the consumer will have to buy additional packs of gum sooner, thus ultimately making your company more money. I don't believe for a second that a family run business would screw the consumer like that, but I just had to throw it out there because my Uncle Bob was right about that Red Dye #5 thing a few years back.

---

264 South Doheny Drive, #8 Beverly Hills, CA 90211

Wm. WRIGLEY Jr. Company

WRIGLEY BUILDING • 410 N. MICHIGAN AVENUE
CHICAGO, ILLINOIS 60611

Telephone: 644-2121
Area Code 312

WHOLESOME • DELICIOUS • SATISFYING

September 17, 2001

Mr. David Paulson
264 Dputh Doheny Drive #8
Beverly Hills, CA 90211
USA

Dear Mr. Paulson:

Thank you for contacting the Wrigley Company to report that you purchased Wrigley gum that was not up to par. Because we want all our consumers to be satisfied with our products, we're glad you took the time to contact us.

Variations in our mixing schedule, a leak in our airtight package or exposure to excessive heat and humidity after it left our factory may have caused your gum to be less than perfect. If you ever come across another pack of Wrigley's gum you aren't completely satisfied with, please send us a few wrapped sticks along with the package wrapper. Our staff will examine them to seek out the cause of the problem, and we'll share their findings with you.

Incidentally, we print a freshness code on the ends of our packages. To help you make sure the Wrigley's gum you buy is fresh, the enclosed sheet explains our product dating.

Although we can't offer a definite explanation, we're sorry the Wrigley's gum you bought wasn't up to standard. To thank you for helping us maintain quality, several fresh packs of Wrigley's gum will soon be on their way to you, with our best wishes.

Sincerely yours,

Consumer Affairs Coordinator

NS/sl
Enclosure

Freshness code dating for Wrigley's gum

To help you make sure the Wrigley's gum you buy is fresh, a number from 1 through 12 representing the month the gum was made is stamped on the ends of each package of our brands. The year of manufacture is indicated by the position of the number, as shown in the diagrams to the right.

Wrigley's gum should remain fresh for up to 12 months after the end code date, depending on the brand. Following is the schedule for each brand:

BRAND	SHELF LIFE
Wrigley's Spearmint®	10 Months
Doublemint®	10 Months
Juicy Fruit®	10 Months
Big Red®	10 Months
Winterfresh®	10 Months
Freedent® Spearmint	10 Months
Freedent® Peppermint	10 Months
Freedent® Winterfresh®	10 Months
Extra® Sugarfree Spearmint	9 Months
Extra® Sugarfree Peppermint	9 Months
Extra® Sugarfree Original Bubble Gum	9 Months
Extra® Sugarfree Classic Bubble Gum	9 Months
Extra® Sugarfree Winterfresh®	9 Months
Extra® Sugarfree Cinnamon	9 Months
Extra® Sugarfree Polar Ice™	9 Months
Eclipse® Sugarfree Spearmint	12 Months
Eclipse® Sugarfree Winterfresh®	12 Months
Eclipse® Sugarfree Polar Ice™	12 Months

Each package of Eclipse® is stamped with a five digit number to the left of the ingredient line. This number represents the manufacture date and can be read as follows: the first two digits represent the month (01-12), the third and fourth digits represent the day (01-31) and the last digit represents the last digit of the year (9=1999, 0=2000, 1=2001). Eclipse® should remain fresh for 12 months after this manufacture date.

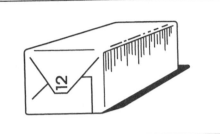

ODD-NUMBERED YEARS
(for example, December 1999, 2001, etc.)

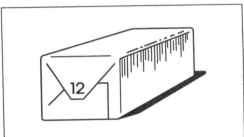

EVEN-NUMBERED YEARS
(for example, December 2000, 2002, etc.)

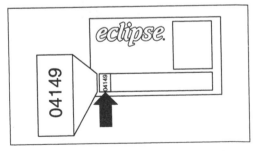

In addition to the package end date, each display box of Wrigley's gum is marked with a "Sell Before" or "Quality Assurance" date. Not only does this help consumers, but it also aids wholesalers and retailers in rotating their stock.

06/00

September 22, 2001

Wm. Wrigley Jr. Company
Wrigley Building
410 North Michigan Avenue
Chicago, Illinois   USA

Dear Sir or Madam:

I hate to say it, but I believe there was a bit of a miscommunication between you and I in regards to my letter dated August 31, 2001.

The JUICYFRUIT gum I contacted you about was not stale or unfresh – it simply lost its flavor in about one minute!! Not just this package, but all packages of JUICYFRUIT. The flavor just doesn't last long at all.

I wonder what your expectations for a stick of JUICYFRUIT gum is supposed to be. How long does the flavor last when <u>you</u> chew it? There must be an answer. Somewhere. Don't you have a lab or something where people test these things?

Secondly, you forwarded me a Freshness Code Dating Chart for Wrigley's Gum that, quite honestly, makes me think I need a college degree in order to decode exactly what you're trying to say on it. Do you offer a Cliff Notes' version of your Freshness Code Dating Chart that you may be able to send me? At least then, I'll get the overview of what you're trying to tell me without having to really read it.

Sincerely,

David Paulson

264 South Doheny Drive, #8 Beverly Hills, CA 90211

September 24, 2001

Best Buy
Consumer Relations
PO Box 9312
Minneapolis, MN 55440

Dear Sir or Madam:

It's currently 12:20PM on September 24, 2001, and I have been on hold with your Los Angeles store for approximately two hours, twelve minutes, and sixteen seconds.

When I originally called at 10:07AM, I asked to speak to someone in the video game department. They transferred me to the TV department instead, and so they had to transfer me back to the front desk. After some time, I asked for the video game department again and they transferred me to the department that handles home appliances. After waiting on hold for sometime in the home appliance department, simply to tell them they sent me to the wrong department, I was transferred to the digital camera department who kept me on hold for another fifteen to twenty minutes, then disregarded what I had to say so they could sing their praises of Sony's current line of digital Cybershot cameras.

Needless to say, I'm still on hold, and may be by the time you receive this letter. But as I'm one of those dedicated people who refuses to give up, I'm definitely not going to give up. But I must tell you it's extremely annoying and this isn't the first time it's happened to me. Last month, I was on hold for fifty-three minutes while someone went to go see if you had any of those Pokemon video games left for my Nintendo 64. When the guy got back on the phone he was chewing, and I believe, had gone out for a bite between looking for my game and getting back to me.

I'm still on hold, even in this paragraph. Isn't there something you guys can do about this?

Loving your on-hold music,

David Paulson

264 South Doheny Drive, #8 Beverly Hills, CA 90211

October 2, 2001

David Paulson
264 South Doheny Drive, Apt. 8
Beverly Hills, CA 90211

Dear Mr. Paulson:

Thank you for investing the time to contact the Best Buy corporate headquarters regarding our customer service. Please allow me to respond accordingly to your concerns.

Let me begin by apologizing on behalf of Best Buy if the level of customer service that you received when calling (attempting to call) our West Los Angeles store failed to meet your expectations. Certainly the experiences that you describe are in no way indicative of the type of service via the telephone that we strive to provide all of our valued customers. Therefore, I have forwarded your comments to the General Manager of store #109. Customer feedback, such as yours, is one of the most important tools that Best Buy has at its disposal to identify opportunities for improvement. Please be assured that we are making every effort to improve the overall level of customer satisfaction and service within all of our stores. I am sincerely sorry and would like to offer an apology for any inconvenience and frustration you experienced as a result of this situation.

In closing, thank you again for taking the time to write. We do appreciate your feedback and look forward to having you back in a Best Buy store very soon!

Sincerely,

Heather Jordan

Heather Jordan
Consumer Relations

CC: General Manager, Best Buy Store #109

October 7, 2001

Consumer Relations
Best Buy
PO Box 9312
Minneapolis, MN 55440

Dear Sir or Madam:

Don't I have egg on my face! As soon as I sent you my last letter, complaining about being kept on hold for over two hours, twelve minutes, and sixteen seconds – somebody picked up the phone and answered my question with poise and good-natured conversation!

When I hung up, you can imagine the distress and depression that overcame me. I remembered back to the time I complained to the Manager of Del Taco for finding half of an earthworm in my chicken quesadilla, resulting in the firing of a worker that, to this day, I refer to as Guillermo. That was the last thing I wanted to happen, in complaining to you.

And so, here I am writing you, in the hopes that you'll be able to stop my letter from causing anyone from getting fired at Best Buy Store #109! In fact, I would greatly appreciate it if you could let me know that I indeed didn't cause the entire staff of Best Buy Store #109 to have to endure one of those condescending "pep talks" that Managers usually give workers who aren't "pulling their weight".

I Best be Buying some more of your products,

David Paulson

264 South Doheny Drive, #8 Beverly Hills, CA 90211

October 15, 2001

David Paulson
264 South Doheny Drive, Apt. 8
Beverly Hills, CA 90211

Dear Mr. Paulson:

Thank you for providing me the opportunity to revisit your concerns regarding our telephone service. Please allow me to address your most recent correspondence.

Thank you for sharing your comments regarding Best Buy's telephone service. It is my understanding that you would like to know if an employee was dismissed due to your previous comments. Employee issues are discussed internally. However, please be assured that no employees were dismissed due to the situation you described in your previous letter.

In closing, thank you again for taking the time to write. We do appreciate your feedback and look forward to having you back in a Best Buy store very soon!

Sincerely,

Heather Jordan
Heather Jordan
Consumer Relations

Best Buy Co., Inc.   7075 Flying Cloud Drive, Eden Prairie, MN 55344 • (952) 947-2000 • NYSE Symbol: BBY

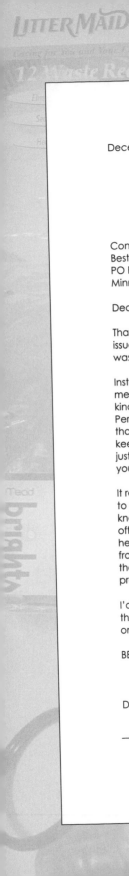

December 11, 2001

Consumer Relations
Best Buy
PO Box 9312
Minneapolis, MN 55440

Dear Sir or Madam:

Thank you for your letter dated October 15th, in which you informed me that "employee issues are discussed internally" and that you preferred not to tell me if one of your staff was fired due to a previous letter I had written.

Instead of that privileged information, I wondered if you'd be able to tell me if the staff members at the Best Buy in Los Angeles had to undergo any kind of seminar or go to any kind of retreat in order to outline to them what proper phone etiquette happens to be? Personally, as I was the customer who had experienced such an issue, I think it's only right that I know if my complaint has been handled, or swept under the rug in an attempt to keep everyone in the dark. People do that, you know. Not just in the government. Not just those guys in the black sedans who threaten you with force. Regular people. Like you and me.

It really all comes down to cause and effect. It's my right to know if a concern I brought to your attention was handled at all. And in having that right, I believe it's my right to know what was done. Did the Manager of the store in question call someone into his office during lunchtime, and (while his mouth was full), tell the employee in question that he "was slacking off" and had better get an "attitude adjustment"? Or did someone from your head office truck on out to the Best Buy in question, (due in part to the fact that my complaint wasn't the ONLY one), and make them sit in front of an overhead projector all day long much like driving school?

I'd appreciate knowing the information as soon as possible. As a customer who spends their money at your store, (over places like Circuit City and The Good Guys), I think it's only fair.

BEST regards,

David Paulson

---

264 South Doheny Drive, #8 Beverly Hills, CA 90211

December 17, 2001

David Paulson
264 South Doheny Drive, #8
Beverly Hills, CA 90211

Dear Mr. Paulson:

Thank you for providing me the opportunity to revisit your concerns regarding our telephone service. Please allow me to address your most recent correspondence.

I understand that you would like to know exactly what happened to the staff at the West Los Angeles store for the poor telephone service you received. However, as per my previous response, all employee issues are dealt with internally. Your comments were forwarded to the General Manager and the District Manager for proper action. I am sincerely sorry for any inconvenience or frustration you have experienced as a result of this situation. Please consider this the sum of my correspondence.

In closing, thank you again for taking the time to write. We do appreciate your feedback and hope you will allow us the opportunity to serve you better in the future.

Sincerely,

Heather Jordan

Heather Jordan
Consumer Relations

Best Buy Co., Inc. 7075 Flying Cloud Drive, Eden Prairie, MN 55344 • (952) 947-2000 • NYSE Symbol: BBY

September 7, 2001

DURKEE MOWER INC.
P.O. Box 470W
Lynn, MA 01903

Dear Sir or Madam:

As a big fan of your Marshmallow Fluff product, and a recent purchaser of a Sharp Carousel Microwave oven, I'm wondering what would happen if I took an entire container of your product, emptied it into a microwave safe bowl, and cooked it on HIGH for about ten minutes.

My friend Elouise tells me that it'll get really big and then I can put it in the freezer and make it into a marshmallow ice-cream pop or something like that, but the scientist part of me says that it's just not possible to make a marshmallow ice-cream pop simply by nuking it in the microwave and freezing it in the freezer.

What do _your_ scientists say?

All about the fluff,

David Paulson

264 South Doheny Drive, #8 Beverly Hills, CA 90211

Marshmallow **fluff**®

DURKEE-MOWER INC.   2 EMPIRE STREET   P.O. BOX 470   LYNN, MASSACHUSETTS 01903-0570   781/593-8007   FAX: 781/593-6410
WEBSITE: HTTP://WWW.MARSHMALLOWFLUFF.COM

September 10, 2001

David Paulson
264 South Doheny Drive #8
Beverly Hills CA 90211

Dear Mr. Paulson:

We would recommend that you follow the scientist part of you that it is not a good idea to nuke Marshmallow Fluff for ten minutes. While we haven't actually experimented with this recipe, our feeling is that after ten mintues it would not need to be frozen but would be a brick of corn syrup and sugar.

We agree with your friend Elouise that the Fluff does get really big and most likely overflow the microwave safe bowl in about one minute. We trust this answers your question.

Very truly yours,

DURKEE-MOWER, INC.

Lynne White

Lynne White

LW:jc

September 22, 2001

Ms. Lynne White
DURKEE MOWER INC.
P.O. Box 470W
Lynn, MA 01903

Dear Ms. White:

You're a life saver! This is going to sound awfully ironic, but as I had already given up on a response from your company, I was just about ready to microwave some Marshmallow Fluff when the mailman delivered your letter to me! I immediately stood down, dropped the Fluff, and called Elouise to let her know that her advice was, in fact, supported by the friendly folks at Durkee Mower, Inc.!

In the heat of the moment, an awfully clever idea came to mind. If my letter possibly represents a thought that thousands of your consumers debate on a daily basis – (i.e. whether or not to microwave Marshmallow Fluff in an attempt to make a large marshmallow ice-pop), then maybe it's something Durkee Mower, Inc. should think about.

I would call it the "MARSHMALLOW MAGIC POP". Think about it – you could sell it in the grocer's freezer and make a killing!! All I ask for in return is a thank you letter and a small picture of me on the back of the packaging with my big THUMBS UP and a little text bubble that reads, "I'm David Paulson, and I'm the inventor of the Marshmallow Magic Pop!" You could drive those Ben & Jerry's kids into the ground with something like that.

What do you think?

Dedicated to making a better ice-pop,

David Paulson
Inventor, Marshmallow Magic Pop

264 South Doheny Drive, #8 Beverly Hills, CA 90211

September 24, 2001

David Paulson
264 S. Doheny Drive #8
Beverly Hills CA 90122

Dear Mr. Paulson:

In response to your recent letter, you can be assured you will be given the appropriate credit for the "Marshmallow Magic Pop" recipe by microwaving Marshmallow Fluff on high for ten minutes.

Very truly yours,

DURKEE-MOWER, INC.

Lynne White

Lynne White

LW:jc

December 10, 2001

Ms. Lynne White
DURKEE MOWER INC.
P.O. Box 470W
Lynn, MA 01903

Dear Ms. White:

With winter quickly on our heels, and snow most likely falling somewhere near your corporate offices, I wanted to drop you a line and wish you the Happiest of Happy Holidays to you and yours.

Since our last correspondence (dated September 24, 2001), a lot has happened with the "MARSHMALLOW MAGIC POP". In fact, you could say that it's "expanded" so large, that it's getting a bit hard to contain these days. Thus my letter, in making sure that the woman who gave me the appropriate credit for said product, knew what was going on before she read about it in "Martha Stewart Living".

In a nutshell, the "David Paulson and Marshmallow Fluff's MARSHMALLOW MAGIC POP" recipe is going to be highlighted in a variety of holiday magazines. These include, "Martha Stewart Living (December 2001 Issue), Vanity Fair (February 2002 Issue), Maxim (January 2002 Issue), and The Truckee Supermarket Times (all next year). In each mention, the magazines will highlight the following recipe:

Marshmallow Fluff's MARSHMALLOW MAGIC POP
1 Container Marshmallow Fluff
1 Microwave
12 Ice Pop Sticks (Or Toothpicks)

Empty an entire container of Durke-Mower's Marshmallow Fluff in a microwave safebowl. Cover loosely with Saran Wrap. Nuke Marshmallow Fluff on HIGH for 10 minutes. Times may vary due to various power discrepancies. When the Fluff has expanded to 10 times its size, quickly remove it and place it in the freezer. After 10 minutes, place the ice pop sticks in various parts of the massive substance. Give it twenty four hours, upon which, remove the substance from the freezer, cutting it into 12 separate magic pops. Walla!

Let me know if you'd like me to send you copies of the magazine articles, of if you'd prefer to just pick them up yourself!

Happy holidays,

David Paulson
Inventor, Marshmallow Magic Pop

264 South Doheny Drive, #8 Beverly Hills, CA 90211

Marshmallow fluff®

DURKEE-MOWER INC.   2 EMPIRE STREET   P.O. BOX 470   LYNN, MASSACHUSETTS 01903-0570   781/593-8007   FAX: 781/593-6410
WEBSITE: HTTP://WWW.MARSHMALLOWFLUFF.COM

December 17, 2001

Mr. David Paulson
264 S. Doheny Drive #8
Beverly Hills, CA 90211

Dear Mr. Paulson:

    Thank you for keeping us posted on the expanded publicity of your "Marshmallow Magic Pop" recipe.
    We would certainly appreciate receiving clips of the various magazine articles for our scrapbook. Again, thank you very much for your efforts.   As a suggestion, you should identify the container size in the recipe as well as the pan size where the microwaved Fluff is deposited.

Very truly yours,

DURKEE-MOWER, INC.

Lynne White
Lynne White

LW:jc

September 10, 2001

Mattel, Inc.
333 Continental Boulevard
El Segundo, CA 90245
Attn: Consumer Relations

Dear Sir or Madam:

I recently purchased your 30th Anniversary UNO game, excited to dive into the fun of a repackaged classic from the last few decades! If you must know, I grew up playing UNO with all of my family and friends, and was often fondly referred to as "the draw four kid" because I frequently was forced to draw four cards over and over and over again.

The reason for my writing your department stems from the inclusion of a "30th Anniversary Card" in the new repackaged UNO. Now, Players with this card are allowed to give all but one of the cards in their hands to another player, thus drastically shortening the game of UNO and sucking a great deal of fun out of long, drawn-out games. My personal nickname has now, unfortunately, evolved into "the guy who always gets all those cards dumped on him thanks to the 30th Anniversary card". I'm half kidding, but you get my point.

Would you be able to tell me why after all these years, you had to go and break a game that didn't need any fixing? I all but threw out my old UNO upon receiving this one, and now wish I could track down those garbage men to return to an UNO I now long for.

The draw four kid,

David Paulson

264 South Doheny Drive, #8 Beverly Hills, CA 90211

September 24, 2001

Mr David Paulson
264 S Doheny Dr #8
Beverly Hills, CA 90211

Dear Mr Paulson:

Thank you for contacting us concerning the Mattel 30th Anniversary Uno. We appreciate the time you have taken to share your thoughts with us.

A great deal of time has gone into the design and manufacture of this item and your disappointment concerns us. Because consumer feedback is very important to us, we have forwarded your comments to the appropriate personnel, here at Mattel, for their interest.

If you should have any questions or concerns about our products in the future, please feel free to call us at 800-567-5437, Monday – Friday, 8:00 am – 6:00 pm, ET.

Sincerely,

Mattel, Inc,
Consumer Relations

Ref. # 8673913

September 11, 2001

Kellogg USA, Inc.
One Kellogg Square
Battle Creek, MI 49107-3599
Attn: Consumer Assistance Department

Dear Sir or Madam:

Let's face it. There's a battle raging out there in consumer America, and it's taking place in the supermarket cereal aisle.

I've remained silent for sometime now, but it's come to the point where I've simply got to express my opinion. And I do hope that your company is open to such direct advice, because in the long run I think you'll find that your customers may have some insight that your executives in suits do not.

Here it is, plain and simple. Frosted Flakes has <u>less</u> sugar in it than Raisin Bran. Did you know that? I'm not quite sure if you did or not. But I looked at the nutrition information just the other day and realized that it was true! For a guy like me who <u>loves</u> Frosted Flakes, it was a dream come true. Forget that crappy, healthy Raisin Bran, that's supposed to keep me regular and put some fruit in my diet! I'd rather eat Frosted Flakes. Hell, it's got <u>less sugar</u> in it than that dehydrated-prune fiber cereal!

I think your consumers would benefit from the above information, and I thought you might want to start a campaign to inform the public about this drastic turn of events. Just off the top of my head, you may want to call it, "The Kellogg's Frosted Flakes is Better than Post Raisin Bran Cereal Due to the Fact That It Has Less Sugar Campaign 2001!"

In the meantime, can you send me one of those holographic Tony the Tiger stickers? I've got a binder just screaming for some low-sugar tiger action!

You're Grrrrrrreat!

David Paulson

264 South Doheny Drive, #8 Beverly Hills, CA 90211

Kellogg's

September 28, 2001

Mr. David Paulson
#8
264 S Doheny Dr.
Beverly Hills, CA 90211

Dear Mr. Paulson:

It was thoughtful of you to take the time to let us know that you enjoy
KELLOGG'S FROSTED FLAKES®. We're always pleased to hear positive comments
from our consumers.

We're happy to have you as part of our consumer family. All of the people at
Kellogg devote a great deal of effort to developing wholesome, appealing
products, and it is good to know that you think we have been successful.

Again, thank you for contacting us; we appreciate your interest in our
company and products.

Sincerely,

Consumer Affairs Department

000000000
KRB/MDA

4573986A

August 29, 2001

Good Humor/Breyers Ice Cream
909 Packerland Drive
Green Bay, WI 54303

Dear Sir or Madam:

I am writing you this letter as a part of your "What Would You Do For A Klondike Bar" contest in which you asked American citizens to tell you about a crazy stunt we've taken part in, solely to receive the world's most wonderful frozen goodie – a Klondike Bar.

When I hear the phrase, "crazy stunt", what often comes to mind is an outdoor stunt of some kind, with very little clothes involved in the scenario. And so, I shed my earthly tweeds and hiked up to the most northern point here in Los Angeles – the Hollywood sign.

There, I spent three days and nights, with only franks and beans to eat. Much like that Brady Bunch episode in which Bobby and Cindy go missing in the Arizona desert – and all they had to eat was franks and beans. Well, that's just what I was going through.

I will say that at the end of three days and nights, most of my body parts were frozen and had very little feeling in them, but knowing that it was all going to result in a Klondike reward, made it way worth my time. I even considered getting arrested for streaking to be "par for the course".

So, what about throwing me some lovin'?

Frozen but happy,

David Paulson

264 South Doheny Drive, #8 Beverly Hills, CA

148

August 28, 2001

Running Press Book Publishers
125 South 22nd Street
Philadelphia, PA 19103-4399
Attn: Customer Service

Dear Sir or Madam:

I recently received The Mini Water Garden Kit as a present for my 30th Birthday.

As your mini-instruction book suggests, The Mini Water Garden Kit contains "everything necessary to recreate the relaxing sound of rippling water wherever it's most needed, whether at home, at work, or on the road." Unfortunately, I have to defiantly disagree.

The Mini Water Garden Kit is frustrating. It is complicated to put together. It contains five tiny little rocks that don't even fill up the little, mini-water trough and are a dangerous choking-hazard for small reptiles, canines, and children. It is absolutely nothing like the larger water gardens I have seen, especially the ones on display at San Francisco's Japanese Water Gardens – which I had the opportunity to experience on my last trip to the "city by the bay". Really, it's quite a wonderful place to go, except for Fisherman's Wharf, where they charge you thirteen-fifty for a crappy little shrimp cocktail.

As for your Mini Water Garden Kit, I feel that your company, Running Press Book Publishers may want to stick to publishing life-size books and accompanying life-size products. What you've gained here in a tiny little novelty item, you've lost in functionality. This product does not relax me, or resemble rippling water whatsoever. It simply makes me wonder who at your company is trying to frustrate those of us who can't afford to buy our own stone water-fountain.

On a totally different note, I noticed you included a poem by Japanese poet Matsuo Basho in the Mini Water Garden mini-book. Although not in the form of a haiku, I sometimes dabble in my own haiku. I thought you might want to put this one on file, in case you publish another mini book of poems. I call it, "Postal Service".

I walk to the street.
And I pick up today's mail.
Will it be from you?

Sincerely,

David Paulson

_____

264 South Doheny Drive, #8 Beverly H

September 10, 2001

The Minute Maid Company
P.O. Box 2079
Houston, TX 77252-2079
Attn: Customer Service

Dear Sir or Madam:

As a big fan of your "Medium Pulp" and "Lots of Pulp" Minute Maid Orange Juice products, I am writing to you in the hopes that an "All Pulp – No Juice" product is very close to being presented to the public at large.

Let me just say, I love pulp. But the problem is, I can't get the quality or quantity of pulp from normal, everyday oranges. I often purchase your "Lots of Pulp" product, drain out the juice into another container, then eat the pulp as a snack. Sometimes, I freeze the pulp I've drained free of juice in small ice-pop containers, and eat them as desserts.

That got me to thinking. An all-pulp (99% juice free) product could be a winner! All I ask for in return of using this ingenious idea is a years supply of the item when it's been fully realized. That's a pretty good deal, don't you think?

Waking up with Minute Maid everday,

David Paulson

264 South Doheny Drive, #8 Beverly Hills, CA 90211

THE **Minute Maid** COMPANY

Consumer Information Center
P.O. Box 2079
Houston, Texas 77252-2079
1-800-888-6488

September 28, 2001

Mr. David Paulson
264 S Doheny Dr Apt 8
Beverly Hills, CA 90211-2593

Dear Mr. Paulson:

Thank you for contacting The Minute Maid Company.

We value your comments and hope that you will use the enclosed coupon to enjoy our products.

Please contact us if we can be of assistance to you in the future.

Sincerely,

Myrna A Martinez

Myrna Martinez
Consumer Response Representative

Ref: 393369

Enclosures: 1 MM Coupon Book

50¢

MANUFACTURER'S COUPON | EXPIRES 12/31/2002

50¢

SAVE 50¢
ON THE PURCHASE OF **ONE**
64 OZ. CARTON OR LARGER

Minute Maid
Premium
ORANGE JUICE

(ANY VARIETY)

09386

An Operating Group of *The Coca-Cola Company*

October 7, 2001

Manager
Consumer Response Center
The Minute Maid Company
P.O. Box 2079
Houston, TX 77252-2079

Dear Sir or Madam:

I hate to be a pest, but it's my belief that when a consumer writes you a letter and poses a particular question, that you should provide an answer if possible.

With that said, I must tell you that I drafted a letter to your company on September 10, 2001 in the hopes that you would be able to tell me whether or not you liked my idea for an "All Pulp" orange juice. A drink that included 99.99% pulp, and 0.01% juice! I've asked around the local supermarkets, and I must say that people seem quite excited about the concept!! Some have even followed up with me to find out when it will be in stores!

However, a certain Ms. Myrna Martinez responded to that letter on September 28th, and for some strange reason, refused to make any mention of my "All Pulp" orange juice idea. It was like I never mentioned it at all. And it got me to wondering why she refused to acknowledge any mention of the ingenious "All Pulp" concept.

Greed. That's why. By now, Ms. Myrna Martinez has probably pitched the idea to your President, has created the product in her own kitchen, and is working her way out of your department and up to a corner office on a very high floor! And it's unfair. So, I wanted you to know exactly where the idea came from, and that Ms. Myrna Martinez is a wolf in sheep's clothing, if I ever saw one!

Waking up with Minute Maid everday,

David Paulson

P.S. – I'd appreciate it if you wouldn't show this letter to Ms. Myrna Martinez.

---

264 South Doheny Drive, #8 Beverly Hills, CA 90211

September 10, 2001

BATTLEBOTS INC.
701 De Long Avenue, Unit K
Novato, CA 94945

Dear Sir or Madam:

I am a big fan of DECIMATOR, a BattleBot who snapped his way to the top and into my heart recently as I watched your show BattleBots on Comedy Central.

Ever since then, I've been working on my own Battlebot that I have named, "SPOON-U-LATOR". "SPOON-U-LATOR" is made up of over 1,000 silver spoons (all taken from various family member's exquisite china collections), then they have been filed so that each spoon has a razor sharp tip. These 1,000 spoons are suspended above the "SPOON-U-LATOR's" spindled wheels which leave room underneath the hanging wall of sharpened spoons for other BattleBots to pass under. When they do, watch out!! The "SPOON-U-LATOR" drops his heavy wall o' spoons onto them, crushing hundreds of little holes inside of them. He's a mean metal eater with a penchant for violence!!

So far, I've only practiced on small toy cars and various pieces of metal, but I think the "SPOON-U-LATOR" is ready for action despite it's size (five feet tall, three feet wide), it's weight (two-hundred twelve pounds), and it's power source (gasoline). I have already made up the T-shirts and it's battle march song, which I call "DANCE OF THE FAIRIES".

What's my next step!? When can I be on the show? Please write me ASAP at the address below.

Let's Get Ready to Rumble!

David Paulson

---

264 South Doheny Drive, #8 Beverly Hills, CA 90211

BattleBots, Inc.
701 DeLong Avenue, Unit K
Novato, CA 94945

9 -15 - 2001

Dear Mr. Paulson,

Thank you for your interest in BattleBots and our competitions.

Upon scrutinized review of your letter, which contains detailed information of your robot, SPOON – U – LATOR, our lawyers have concluded that competitors cannot utilize stolen parts on their robots and compete in our show. We understand that you have "taken" your spoons for the weapon without written consent of your various family members. We at BattleBots, however, are intrigued with your spoon design and have decided to help so that your robot will be eligible to compete.

BattleBots, Inc. has decided to donate to you 1,000 plastic spoons from our "china collection" making them legitimate parts. Since they are plastic you may need to find a new way to file them for your "wall o' spoons" weapon.

We wish you luck on your endeavor and hope you will compete in our next show!

Remember, " safety first "

Sincerely,
BattleBots, Inc.

701 DeLong Avenue, Unit K • Novato, CA • 94945-3224 • T: (415) 898-7522 • F: (415) 898-7525 • info@battlebots.com • www.battlebots.com

154

December 13, 2001

Mr. Andy Puzder
CEO
Carl's Jr.
401 West Carl Karcher Way
P.O. Box 4349
Anaheim, CA 92803

Dear Mr. Puzder:

As a volunteer in a local rest home, I can't tell you how disgusting it is to watch people who have trouble keeping food in their mouths, eat an entire meal. That's why, as I'm sure you can imagine, I also found it quite hard to watch your TV commercials that lauded your catch phrase, "If it doesn't get all over the place, it doesn't belong in your face".

Which brings me to why I'm writing you this letter. As I'm currently taking night classes in Marketing, I have reached the point in the semester where I must turn in my thesis paper. This term, it just happens to be about your company's advertising campaign.

Entitled "Carl's Jr. and A Catch Phrase That Has Absolutely Nothing To Do With The Quality of Their Food, While Disgusting Rest Home Employees at the Same Time", is currently a work-in-progress, but is due at the beginning of January 2002. I have found that in order to provide both sides of the argument, it has become absolutely necessary for me to secure a letter from you about the above campaign. If you'd be so kind as to answer the following questions, I'd greatly appreciate it.

- Why is a messy meal, a good thing?
- What is it about staining white dress shirts with ketchup that appeals to the American public?
- Is the advertising firm that developed the above concept, still employed by your corporation, or have they been fired and sent on their merry own way?

I'd be extremely pleased if, along with the above answers, you might forward me a signed head shot of yourself that I may use for the cover of my paper. I plan on dripping various kinds of condiments on the picture, hoping that the mess will both make a point and quite possibly (if you know something I don't) get me an A.

Please don't use this letter as a napkin,

David Paulson

---

264 South Doheny Drive, #8 Beverly Hills, CA 90211

CKE RESTAURANTS

3916 STATE STREET • SUITE 300
SANTA BARBARA, CALIFORNIA 93105
805-898-4228

December 21, 2001

Mr. David Paulson
264 S. Doheny Dr. #8
Beverly Hills, CA 90211

Dear Mr. Paulson,

Thank you for taking the time to comment on our advertising. Your feedback is important to us and we regret that you were displeased with the ad you saw.

Our ad is designed to give the viewer an idea of what a truly great burger experience is like and, as you may know, eating a big, juicy, delicious burger such as ours may involve getting a little messy. Not like the skimpy, little burgers served at other places.

This series of commercials is meant to be viewed as humorous and lighthearted, but sometimes humor can be a very subjective business. We are truly sorry if you took offense, regardless of our intentions, and sincerely hope you will find our upcoming commercials to be more to your liking.

Sincerely,

Peter B. Espinosa, Jr.
Guest Relations

CARL'S JR. • HARDEE'S

156

October 2, 2001

Friskies Consumer Service Center
P.O. Box 2178
Wilkes Barre, PA 18703

Dear Sir or Madam:

Mister Tinkle-Puss absolutely loves your cat food, and as a result of his incessant purring and clatter lately, I am writing you this letter to communicate his thoughts.

In fact, he so loves your FRISKIES cat food, that it got me to wondering just how it tasted. So what did this crazy human do? He tasted a tablespoon of it. And I have to admit, It wasn't half bad.

So, here's my question. You know how they're always telling you to have water and canned food on hand in case of an earthquake (at least out here in the West)? If I ended up eating all my canned food in a disaster situation, would it be un-healthful to eat Mister Tinkle-Puss' FRISKIES cat food? I mean, is there a reason why human's shouldn't eat it? I'd love to know the answer.

Purrrrfectly in good taste,

David Paulson

P.S. – Just for your info, ALPO dog food does not taste good. It sort of tastes like a mix between Elmer's Glue and liver.

264 South Doheny Drive, #8 Beverly Hills, CA 90211

Friskies PetCare Company, Inc.

Consumer Services Center
P.O. Box 2178
Wilkes-Barre, PA 18703
1-800-555-3747
www.friskies.com

October 5, 2001

Mr. David Paulson
264 S Doheny Dr
Apt 8
Beverly Hills, CA 90211-2538

Dear Mr. Paulson,

Thank you for contacting us about FRISKIES Canned Cat Food. We welcome questions and comments from our consumers.

Although our pet food/treat products are of food grade quality and there are no harmful ingredients in them, they are not for human consumption. The label states very clearly that the product is for a dog/cat.

At Friskies PetCare Company, we are committed to the well being of cats and dogs. We continually strive to make the highest quality pet food products to ensure that cats and dogs receive the most nutritious diets to keep them healthy and happy. We are very dedicated to quality in all aspects of our business.

We value you as a customer and appreciate your use of our products. If we can be of further assistance, please do not hesitate to contact us, Monday through Friday, 8 a.m. to 8 p.m., Eastern Time.

Sincerely,

Friskies PetCare Expert

Ref: 7160700

P.S. We invite you to visit us online - your resource for healthy and happy pets. At VeryBestPet.com, you'll find information and helpful tips on pet health, behavior, grooming, preventative care and much more. For product related information, please visit us any time at Friskies.com.

December 10, 2001

Friskies Pet Care Expert
Consumer Services Center
P.O. Box 2178
Wilkes Barre, PA 18703

Dear Friskies Pet Care Expert:

Thank you for your letter dated October 5th, 2001. I appreciated how quickly you responded to my initial question about whether or not it was safe for humans to ingest your FRISKIES product.

I do understand that "the label states very clearly that the product is for a dog/cat" and that "they are not for human consumption."   However, I have a hypothetical question for you.

What would you tell a person who had <u>mistakenly</u> ingested a can of FRISKIES a day, for three months straight? Don't ask me how someone could ingest that much cat food for that long a time period – this is a hypothetical question. But hypothetically, what would you tell someone who had done that?

Your answer would be greatly appreciated in a timely manner as I would like to share the information with a person very close to me.

Thank you,

David Paulson

264 South Doheny Drive, #8 Beverly Hills, CA 90211

Friskies PetCare Company, Inc.

Consumer Services Center
P.O. Box 2178
Wilkes-Barre, PA 18703
1-800-555-3747
www.friskies.com

December 14, 2001

Mr. David Paulson
264 S Doheny Dr
Apt 8
Beverly Hills, CA 90211-2538

Dear Mr. Paulson,

Thank you for contacting us about FRISKIES Canned Cat Food. We welcome questions and comments from our consumers.

At Friskies PetCare Company, we are committed to the well being of cats and dogs. We continually strive to make the highest quality pet food products to ensure that cats and dogs receive the most nutritious diets to keep them healthy and happy. We are very dedicated to quality in all aspects of our business.

Although our pet food/treat products are of food grade quality and there are no harmful ingredients in them, they are not for human consumption. The label states very clearly that the product is for a dog/cat.

We value you as a customer and appreciate your use of our products. We invite you to use the enclosed savings toward your next purchase. If we can be of further assistance, please do not hesitate to contact us, Monday through Friday, 8 a.m. to 8 p.m., Eastern Time.

Sincerely,

Friskies PetCare Expert

Ref: 7355445
enclosure
P.S. We invite you to visit us online - your resource for healthy and happy pets. At VeryBestPet.com, you'll find information and helpful tips on pet health, behavior, grooming, preventative care and much more. For product related information, please visit us any time at Friskies.com.

December 13, 2001

Hertz Rent-A-Car
225 Brae Boulevard
Park Ridge, NJ 07656
Attn: Customer Service

Dear Sir or Madam:

As the Paulson Family's Annual "Across The County In As Many Days As It Takes Us To Do It In" Car Speed-A-Thon is rapidly approaching (February 2002), I decided it would be a good idea to contact your head office in advance, in an attempt to determine whether or not your corporation has the ability to provide us with what we need.

February's Annual Car Speed-A-Thon is going to be the biggest one yet. With my family (6), my brother's family (8), my brother's best-friend's family (4), the grandparents (8), the aunts and uncles (5), and the Mayor of Santa Monica and his constituents (15), we're looking at about a grand total of 46 people!! That's ten more people than last year, and it means were going to have to print way more t-shirts and headbands than we originally thought. It also means we're going to need cars. A lot of cars.

Being based in the Southern California area, we're going to need you to find us a satellite office that can provide us with enough four-wheel drive SUVs and trucks that can handle mountainous terrain, slick road conditions; that come with DVD players and TV monitors, FM/AM/CD stereo systems, built in trays for eating meals, and chains for tires in snowy conditions. On top of that, they must come with gas. Gas is key. Enough gas to take us to New York City.

We plan on having drivers above the age of 25 piloting each car as it wings its way across the country. There is one exception, however -- my brother's eldest Frank, who just got his permit license, and who will be practicing his driving with his dad by his side as we cross the Rocky Mountains.

As we're set to ship off on February 1st, 2002, I'll need to know fairly soon if you'll be able to provide us with such a tall order.

Truckin',

David Paulson

P.S. – Is it true that you make your employees actually <u>wash</u> your cars? Cause to me, that seems a little, well, like fraternity hazing.

264 South Doheny Drive, #8 Beverly Hills, CA 90211

The Hertz Corporation
6151 W. Century Blvd., Ste. 600, Los Angeles, CA 90045
Telephone: (310) 568-5100

January 7, 2002

Dear Mr. Paulson,

We have read your letter and proposed travel. Hertz would like to provide you with the necessary vehicles for your trip. Please contact us to discuss the details of your trip.

Sincerely,

Brian Becker

(310) 568-2648

September 27, 2001

Ms. Martha Stewart
Martha Stewart Living Omnimedia LLC
20 West 43rd Street
New York, New York 10036

Dear Ms. Stewart:

Let me be completely straightforward and honest when I tell you that I think you've been getting a bad rap lately. From Saturday Night Live to magazine articles and Internet discussion boards – people are wondering aloud if you're simply a dishonest, conniving, businesswoman.

You know what I say!? I say, screw them all! In fact, what's so bad about being dishonest and conniving if you're making money in the process!? And on top of that, if you're also helping normal everyday people learn how to craft objects of household beautification out of acorns and popcorn kernels – you're way ahead of the curve if you ask me.

I say, forget about them Ms. Stewart. Don't let them ruffle your feathers. Simply remember that the Universe is a gigantic expanding "something" that is quite possibly infinite (as Carl Sagan says), and when you hold your little, meaningless, insignificant life against a backdrop like that – none of any of this matters at all! None of it!

Kindest regards,

David Paulson

P.S. – I have figured out a way to make a decorate garbage disposal cap out of tree branches and petrified mushrooms. I call it, the "Decorative Garbage Disposal Mushroom Cap", in case you'd like to highlight it in an upcoming article or TV program.

October 19, 2001

Mr. David Paulson
264 South Doheny Dr. #8
Beverly Hills, CA 90211

Dear Mr. Paulson,

Thank you for your recent correspondence. Please know that your comments and suggestions are welcome, and have been forwarded to Martha Stewart and appropriate members of the *Living* staff.

Your letter will remain in our files for future reference. We do appreciate your taking the time to write in, and hope you will continue to enjoy Martha's work.

Best wishes to you.

Sincerely,

Martha Stewart Living
Customer Relations

December 11, 2001

Customer Relations
Martha Stewart Living Omnimedia LLC
20 West 43rd Street
New York, New York 10036

Dear Customer Relations:

Your letter dated October 19th, 2001 stated that my "comments and suggestions are welcome, and have been forwarded to Martha Stewart…".

What exactly does that mean? I would appreciate knowing how this transpired. Did someone copy the letter, then put it in Ms. Stewart's in-box on her desk? Or did my letter never get to her and you're simply telling me that so I won't write back to you again?

I find it extremely hard to believe that somewhere in New York, Martha Stewart is sitting in her limo, or out back on a hand-crafted bench made out of a dried-pumpkin, reading through my comments and suggestions so that she can, someday, write back to me. In fact, will anyone <u>ever</u> find the time to write back to me and give me their thoughts on my "Decorative Garbage Disposal Mushroom Cap"? Because if Martha gives the thumbs up on it, I can pump out about twenty-two of those a day. I could start my own business.

So, you can imagine the importance I put on hearing back from your staff or the illustrious Ms. Stewart.

Kindest regards,

David Paulson

264 South Doheny Drive, #8 Beverly Hills, CA 90211

September 11, 2001

Helene Curtis
Consumer Service Department
800 Sylvan Avenue
Englewood Cliffs, NJ 07632

Dear Sir or Madam:

I became aware of a very serious situation the other evening while at dinner with a group of my friends. All of us, having just finished wolfing down a plate of sushi and green tea ice cream, began talking about the products we use on a daily basis in making ourselves attractive and pretty for the opposite sex.

Needless to say, your product FINESSE came up. And the most depressing results of said conversation was...none of us have purchased your shampoo/conditioner product in over a decade.

Some were using PRELL, while others have moved on to shampoos that come from other countries, smell like mangos, or make your hair tingle like you dipped your head in a vat of Junior Mints. That's when I got to thinking about why your consumer base has most likely dropped over the years, and it came down to one thing. Your jingle.

Do you remember, "Sometime you use a little... Sometimes you use a lot. Sometimes you use a little FINESSE... Sometimes you use a LOT!"? See, for me, upon hearing that jingle I honestly thought to myself that Helene Curtis was a pretty upstanding company, offering its consumer the option to use a little, OR use a lot! And while other shampoo companies suggested "lathering a large amount of shampoo" in ones' hair (simply a ploy to have consumers use it up quicker and buy another container of it), Helene Curtis was doing their part in not pushing the issue. Simply giving consumers, "a choice".

You'll be glad to know that upon reminding the rest of my friends at the dinner table exactly what I just told you – it was like a fog of depression was lifted off of them. They realized what they were doing wrong. And I'm happy to say that we all went out that night to a 24 hour 7-ELEVEN to purchase a bottle of your FINESSE Shampoo & Conditioner.

What do you have to say about that!

I'm Going To Use A Little, Or A Lot!

David Paulson

264 South Doheny Drive, #8 Beverly Hills, CA 90211

HELENE
CURTIS

Telephone 1-800-621-2013

September 26, 2001

Mr. David Paulson   EF 1184637A
264 South Doheny Drive #8
Beverly Hills, CA 90211

Dear Mr. Paulson:

Thank you for sharing your thoughts about Finesse Shampoo and Conditioner. Our corporate goal is "meeting the everyday needs of people everywhere". It is truly rewarding when our consumers feel strongly about our brands and take the time to communicate with us directly.

Our goal has always been to provide consumers with the finest products that scientific research and human skills can develop. A personal commendation such as yours is most welcome and greatly appreciated. It assures us that we are achieving our goal. We will be pleased to share your comments with the appropriate staff.

We sincerely appreciate your taking the time to contact us and hope you enjoy the enclosed. If you have any additional questions or comments, please call us at our toll free number or visit our web site at www.unilever800.com.

Sincerely,

Kim Wilson
Consumer Representative

KW/RMB
Enclosures

October 5, 2001

Mr. Ken Kim
President
Medieval Times
7662 Beach Boulevard
Buena Park, CA 90620

Dear Mr. Kim:

I'm writing this letter in the hopes that your Medieval Times Restaurant happens to be looking for a Black Knight for your jousting tournament and dinner show.

Having trained with a man who calls himself, "Abhor of Cullins", I spent many a years on the Rennassaince Fair circuit, training in the arts of joust, sword-play, and most importantly…scaring young children with my evil stares. In the real world it's laughable, I know, but in the world of Medieval Times, it's bone-chilling.

After graduating from "Assistant to the Black Knight, Abhor of Cullins", I moved up to the rank of "Black Knight of Gorlan" with my official fighting name becoming "Kulack of Gorlan". I have all the regulation Black Knight armor, swords, and I sometimes dabble in writing my own evil dialogue… although I'm sure your shows are already scripted by some very talented people.

Please let me know if there are any current openings for a Black Knight such as myself, as soon as possible. I'm fielding a few other offers, one at Epcot Center's brand-new "Knights", as well as forming my own corporation and doing parties and dances on my own. I'd appreciate some kind of response so if, need be, I can move onto my less desirable options.

Hear-ye, hear-ye,

David Paulson
(a.k.a. The Black Knight of Gorlan)

264 South Doheny Drive, #8 Beverly Hills, CA 90211

Medieval Times
DINNER & TOURNAMENT

Medieval Times is a DRUG FREE environment!
Pre-employment DRUG TESTING IS REQUIRED!

APPLICATION FOR EMPLOYMENT – All applicants will receive consideration for employment without regard to Race, Color, Religion, Sex, Age, National Origin, Marital Status, Physical Handicap, Veteran Status, Disability, Medical Condition, Ancestry or any other consideration made unlawful by federal, state or local laws.

PERSONAL

PLEASE PRINT – ALL INFORMATION WILL BE TREATED CONFIDENTIALLY

INCOMPLETE APPLICATIONS MAY NOT BE CONSIDERED

NAME: _____
　　　　Last　　　　　First　　　　　Initial

HOME PHONE: ( )　　　　MESSAGE PHONE: ( )

ADDRESS: _____
　　　　Number　　　Street　　　City　　　State　　　Zip

SOCIAL SECURITY NUMBER: _____

APPLYING FOR:
☐ CASH CONTROL　☐ PHOTO　　☐ BAR SERVICE
☐ GIFT SHOP　　☐ MAINTENANCE　☐ FOOD SERVICE　☐ SHOW
　　　　　　　☐ OFFICE/CLERICAL　☐ SECURITY　☐ OTHER

THE CASTLE IS OPEN SEVEN DAYS A WEEK, INCLUDING ALL HOLIDAYS

WILL YOU WORK:
DAY SHIFT:　☐ YES　☐ NO
EVENING SHIFT:　☐ YES　☐ NO

MON	☐ YES	☐ NO
TUES	☐ YES	☐ NO
WED	☐ YES	☐ NO
THURS	☐ YES	☐ NO
FRI	☐ YES	☐ NO
SAT	☐ YES	☐ NO
SUN	☐ YES	☐ NO

WHEN WILL YOU BE AVAILABLE FOR WORK? _____ Wages Expected _____

I UNDERSTAND THAT DUE TO SCHEDULE REQUIREMENTS, I CANNOT BE GUARANTEED TO WORK DAYS OR SHIFT I WAS ORIGINALLY HIRED FOR.

IF YOU ARE NOT A U.S. CITIZEN, CAN YOU SUBMIT PROOF OF LEGAL RIGHT TO WORK IN THIS COUNTRY AFTER AN OFFER OF EMPLOYMENT? ☐ YES ☐ NO

ARE YOU UNDER 18? ☐ YES ☐ NO IF UNDER 18, DATE OF BIRTH _____ IF HIRED, YOU MAY BE REQUIRED TO FURNISH PROOF THAT YOUR AGE MEETS LEGAL REQUIREMENTS

HAVE YOU EVER BEEN CONVICTED OF A CRIME? EXCLUDE TRAFFIC VIOLATIONS. A CONVICTION RECORD DOES NOT NECESSARILY DISQUALIFY YOU FROM EMPLOYMENT. ANY RELATIONSHIP BETWEEN THE JOB YOU ARE SEEKING AND THE OFFENSE WILL BE TAKEN INTO ACCOUNT ALONG WITH OTHER RELEVANT FACTORS. ☐ YES ☐ NO IF YES, PLEASE EXPLAIN:

DO YOU HAVE ANY PHYSICAL OR MEDICAL RESTRICTION WHICH MAY LIMIT YOUR ABILITY TO PERFORM THE JOB APPLIED FOR? ☐ YES ☐ NO IF YES, EXPLAIN:

PLEASE INDICATE ANY ACCOMMODATIONS THE COMPANY MUST MAKE WHICH WOULD MAKE IT POSSIBLE FOR YOU TO PERFORM THE JOB:

DO YOU HAVE ANY RELATIVES EMPLOYED AT THIS COMPANY? ☐ YES ☐ NO (IF YES, WHOM?)

HAVE YOU EVER WORKED FOR MEDIEVAL TIMES BEFORE? ☐ YES ☐ NO IF YES, LOCATION, DATES & POSITION HELD:

WHERE DID YOU LEARN OF THIS POSITION? _____

IF BY NEWSPAPER OR AGENCY, GIVE NAME _____

REFERENCES

LIST TWO NAMES (DO NOT INCLUDE RELATIVES, FORMER EMPLOYERS)

NAME	ADDRESS	PHONE	OCCUPATION	HOW LONG KNOWN

August 28, 2001

Krispy Kreme Doughnut Corporation
370 Knollwood, Ste. 500
Winston-Salem, NC 27103

Dear Sir or Madam:

Let me start by saying that I weighed 180 pounds before I ever heard of Krispy Kreme. Now, ten months later, after a Krispy Kreme opened up just down the street from my office in Van Nuys, California – I weight 258. As you can tell, I'm a "big" fan.

In an effort to know as much as possible about the corporation who forced me to buy a whole new set of slacks, I stumbled upon your COLLECTIBLES STORE on your website. There, I was amazed to find out that Krispy Kreme didn't just sell donuts! They sold t-shirts, and sweatshirts, caps, mugs, boxer-shorts, and small little trucks for children everywhere! But sadly, I was surprised at the lack of diversity presented therein. Especially, by a company who obviously goes out of their way to staff their stores with a diverse group of doughnut technicians.

As a child, I spent a lot of time around ethnic individuals. Black, yellow, white, off-white… I rode the bus with them, went to school with them, drank water out of the same water fountains as them. And I came to the conclusion that although we were all very different in our histories and family backgrounds, there was one commonality between us all. Our love of music.

I believe that by embracing the one common interest between all people of this great Planet Earth, Krispy Kreme would jump leaps and bounds ahead of such anti-diverse companies as Winchell's and Bob's Donuts, by creating a toy that communicates to the children (all habits are formed in childhood), that this world is only what we make of it.

And so, "The Whistling Donut" was born. Made as a replica, in plastic, of a jelly-filled doughnut, it would in reality be a fully-functional flute! By placing fingers over various jelly oozing holes, people will be able to play a variety of songs, inspired by their heritage! And on top of that, Krispy Kreme Corp. could possibly create their own theme song, with instructions how to play it included inside the plastic doughnut! Maybe even employing a group like Blink 182 or The Red Hot Chili Peppers to write such a song would suck in those Generation X'ers.

I'd love to hear your thoughts, and I also want you to know that I polled the people in my apartment complex, and they say that they'd travel to Van Nuys to buy "The Whistling Donut" and might even pick up a dozen or so doughnuts while they were there!

One "big" fan,

David Paulson

264 South Doheny Drive, #8 Beverly Hills, CA 90211

David Paulson
264 South Doheny Drive #8
Beverly Hills, CA 90211

Thank you for your letter and interest in Krispy Kreme Doughnuts. We appreciate your feedback. Please be advised that we are unable to accept ideas for commercials, marketing strategies and the like. In order to protect our right to develop our own ideas, we cannot accept or review ideas of this nature.

However, we do greatly appreciate your interest in Krispy Kreme and your enthusiasm for our products!

Best regards,

http://www.krispykreme.com

Krispy Kreme Doughnut Corporation
Post Office Box 83, Winston-Salem, NC 27102, Tel (336) 725-2981, Fax (336) 733-3791, www.krispykreme.com

171

September 22, 2001

Krispy Kreme Doughnut Corporation
370 Knollwood, Ste. 500
Winston-Salem, NC 27103

Dear Krispy Kreme:

I wanted to drop you a quick note of thanks for your quick reply to my letter regarding my idea for the Krispy Kreme "Whistling Doughnut". I understand and appreciate your honestly, in telling me that your company cannot accept or review ideas of this nature.

I did want to let you know that in the time between writing you my first letter, and receiving yours, I created a prototype of the "Whistling Doughnut" with my friend Hal. Hal is a prominent plastic molding engineer, and works at a local Hollywood costume shop where he creates those ghoul masks that were all the rage back in the early 90's.

Let me tell you this. The "Whistling Doughnut" is a success! So far, Hal and I have been able to play such songs on the "Whistling Doughnut" as 'When The Saints Go Marching In', 'Every Rose Has Its Thorn', and "Baby's Got Back". Really, it sounds just like the original versions of those songs! You'd have a hard time discerning between my version and theirs.

As you can't review this idea, I wondered if you could <u>at least</u> tell me if you think I'm on the right track with the product. Would you buy something like this, from an independent company, such as the one I'm about to create? Or do you think it's a waste of time and maybe should I get back into my old business of telephone soliciting for a portable adult diaper distributer?

Also, I wondered… as an employee of Krispy Kreme, do you get free doughnuts and coffee everyday? Cause if they don't, you should really spearhead some kind of sit-in or stage some kind of demonstration. I mean, c'mon, those doughnuts are cheap to make!

Whistling a tune,

David Paulson

---

264 South Doheny Drive, #8 Beverly Hills, CA 90211

December 10, 2001

Customer Service Manager
Krispy Kreme Doughnut Corporation
370 Knollwood, Ste. 500
Winston-Salem, NC 27103

Dear Sir or Madam:

Let me first start off by telling you I'm a big fan of Krispy Kreme doughnuts. Many a time (after eating eight to ten of your product in a quick-like fashion) I find myself feeling strange or dizzy in a good way, which always keeps me coming back for more. Krispy Kreme does what no other doughnut company can do – and whatever it is, I'm buying it one-hundred percent!

An area where Krispy Kreme does need some help, unfortunately, is in the Customer Service area. After writing a letter to your company back in August, proposing what I like to call "The Whistling Doughnut", a staff member of yours who preferred to remain anonymous seemingly stole my idea after telling me he was uninterested in using it.

Some background on "The Whistling Doughnut". Created this year by myself and my friend Hal (a prominent plastic molding engineer), the product resembles a Krispy Kreme doughnut but is in reality...a working musical instrument!! Hal and myself have already worked up charts for various songs that can be played on this lyrical wonder, like "When The Saints Go Marching In", "The Star Spangled Banner", and "Baby's Got Back". Unfortunately, the success of "The Whistling Doughnut" is now in question, as your unnamed staff member is already twisting his black-gloved evil hands in satisfaction – knowing that we have no control over where or what he does with this idea.

We did not sign any release forms. We did not have any meetings with your President. But here we are, sitting helpless, as one unnamed customer service representative decides our fate. That's why I'm writing to you, the unnamed Boss of the unnamed staff member, so you can put a stop to this before you get dragged down into an embroiled legal battle the likes of which none of us have ever seen before.

Whistling a happy tune,

David Paulson

264 South Doheny Drive, #8 Beverly Hills, CA 90211

January 4, 2002

Mr. Donald Paulson
264 South Doheny Drive, #8
Beverly Hills, CA 90211

Dear Mr. Paulson:

Our purpose in revealing to you that we were not accepting detailed descriptions of ideas was in response to overwhelming unsolicited recommendations. While it is truly an honor that you and others feel strongly that we would be good partners in your enterprises, we are best able to serve our customers by using in-house resources and market research to manage additions and changes to our look and product lines.

I wish you much success as you develop your whistle project.

Sincerely,

Krispy Kreme Doughnut Corporation

Director Customer Experience

SA/kw

Krispy Kreme Doughnut Corporation
Post Office Box 83, Winston-Salem, NC 27102, Tel (336) 725-2981, Fax (336) 733-3791, www.krispykreme.com

174

October 5, 2001

Mr. Robert C.W. Ettinger
Cryonics Institute
24355 Sorrentino Court
Clinton Township, MI 48035

Dear Mr. Ettinger:

I apologize that it's taken me so long to write you, but I wanted to commend you on that wonderfully interesting Internet chat you did with ABCNews.com back in February 2001.

As an avid fan of ice and all things cold, I have been thinking a lot lately about spending my twilight years in a cryogenic state. Unfortunately, I'm a bit concerned about the damage that could possibly be done to my system by freezing it.

I don't know if you saw that ABC Special where that magician David Blaine froze himself in a big block of ice – but when he got out of there, he could barely even form words or sentences! The last thing I want is to wake up in the year 2150 and not be able to tell people my name. Or ask them for a Cheeseburger! Hell, they could be force-feeding me futuristic glop, when all I wanted was a slab of beef but just couldn't vocalize that to them. Not fun, Mr. Ettinger. Not fun at all.

In addition to my above concern, I wondered what the cost would be to freeze my body. If it's pricey, I may just want to freeze my head instead, but then that makes me wonder what I'll do for a body when I awaken. All valid questions, I'm sure. And as you're the expert, I'd love it if you could shed some light on the subject.

Cold as ice, someday!

David Paulson

CRYONICS INSTITUTE

24355 Sorrentino Court
Clinton Township, MI 48035
Phone (810) 791-5961
Fax(810) 792-7062

Greetings:

Enclosed is the Cryonics Institute sign-up pack that you requested. If you need more copies, and do not have access to a copy machine, you can request more from the institute.

Also enclosed is the most recent issue of *The Immortalist*. If you are interested in a subscription, the form and rates are on the back cover.

If you have any questions, do not hesitate to call, write, or email. My email address is CIHQ@aol.com.

Sincerely,

Andy Zawacki
Facility Manager

New Membership Option

At the annual meeting September 27, 1998, the CI members approved an additional option for membership.

CI until then had offered a single membership plan, including the following features (slightly simplified here for succinctness): A one-time up-front membership fee of $1,250; no dues, except for those who want voting rights-voting rights dues now $100/year; minimum suspension fee of $28,000.

However, even though the total costs are far less than in other organizations, some prospective members have very limited cash available. These include some students and some older people living on fixed incomes. Yet many students can afford life insurance, and many older people can fund a suspension out of assets available at death, including real estate. Further, some people simply prefer to part with as little cash as possible at a given time. Certainly a decision is easier when very little cash is required.

So we now offer an alternative-Membership Option Two.

PLEASE NOTE CAREFULLY that Option Two does NOT replace the previous Option One. Present members are not affected at all, nor is the status of existing contracts. Option Two is just an alternative for consideration by prospective new members.

Either the new option (Option Two) or the older option (Option One) is now available to new members. Option Two allows membership in CI and execution of a contract with the smallest initial cash outlay available anywhere, as well as minimal total cost. Option Two has the following features:

There is no membership fee.

Dues (payable in advance) are $120 per year or $35 quarterly. The first payment secures your current membership and the right to execute a contract. If dues are not paid when owing, membership lapses and contracts are not in force.

Minimum suspension fee is $35,000, whole body.

If the Option Two member wants voting rights, and the right to stand for office, there are voting dues of $100 per year additional. Voting dues for Option Two members must be paid for three years before eligibility to vote or hold office.

Option Two members may switch to Option One at any time by paying the $1,250 Option One membership fee.

October 22, 2001

Mr. Andy Zawacki
Facility Manager
Cryonics Institute
24355 Sorrentino Court
Clinton Township, MI 48035

Dear Mr. Zawacki:

Although I greatly appreciated the packet of information you sent me based on my original letter, I'm still quite concerned about what I'm going to do for a body after I freeze my head in a cryogenic chamber.

I'm sure there's no concrete answer to my above query, but as the Facility Manager, I figured you'd have some experience in at least, coming up with some kind of answer. I mean, you are the Facility Manager.

So, I'd greatly appreciate it, Mr. Zawacki, if you could respond to this letter and alleviate my concerns in regards to solely freezing my head and leaving my body here in the 21st Century.

Cool-headed,

David Paulson

264 South Doheny Drive, #8 Beverly Hills, CA 90211

August 30, 2001

Mr. Ben Cohen & Mr. Jerry Greenfield
Ben & Jerry's Homemade Holdings, Inc.
30 Community Drive
South Burlington, VT 05403-6828

Dear Ben & Jerry:

You guys are crazy! Some would say certifiable! The way in which you combine candy and ice cream and cookies into a swirl of mouth-watering heaven! What's next!!?

I'll tell you. This flavor, which I have tested and tasted thousands of times in the privacy of my own home is called "JEW CREW". It combines vanilla and chocolate fudge ice cream with halvah (a Jewish/Middle Eastern sweet sesame candy), coconut (think Macaroons), chocolate covered raspberry jellies, and pieces of chocolate fudge. All of the items are traditional candies from the Jewish culture and would make for a tasty and popular combination. You could even include yarmulkes with Special Edition Pints of the ice cream as a neat little souvenir.

What do you think?

Shalom,

David Paulson

September 13, 2001

David Paulson
264 South Doheny Dr.
#8
Beverly Hills, CA 90211

Dear David:

Thank you for sharing your creativity with us! Some of our best-selling flavors were suggested by consumers just like you, including Cherry Garcia., Chubby Hubby. and Chunky Monkey.! Before we're able to consider your idea and share it with others at Ben & Jerry's, we need you to agree to a few terms; otherwise, it will just sit in our files here in the Consumer Affairs department. Please pardon our formality. Our legal department says that in all fairness, we must let everyone know what our acceptance policy is all about. We can't do anything these days without the lawyers getting involved!

Enclosed is the "Ben & Jerry's Agreement and Policy Concerning Suggestions". Please read through it and if you accept and agree to everything that is written, sign the last page and send it back to us using the enclosed postage-paid return envelope. If you're under the age of 18, please review the policy with your parents or guardian and have them sign it with you. If we don't receive your signed agreement within a reasonable length of time, we'll assume you don't want us to consider your idea and in our files it will stay, never to be shared with others. Such a shame!

If you have access to the internet, you can send us your idea using the "Suggestion Box" in the Consumer Assistance section of our website. We're at www.benjerry.com. Check us out!

Thanks for caring and taking the time to write us. If you have any questions, please give us a call at (802) 846-1500 between 9:00a.m. and 5:00p.m. EST Monday through Friday. Ask for Consumer Affairs. If we decide to use your idea, you'll be hearing from us!

Flavorably Yours,

Ben & Jerry's

Enc.

30 Community Drive • South Burlington, Vermont • 05403-6828 • Tel: 802/846-1500 • www.benjerry.com

BEN & JERRY'S AGREEMENT AND
POLICY CONCERNING SUGGESTIONS

This Agreement sets forth the terms and conditions you agree to before we may consider for development the suggestion you recently sent to Ben & Jerry's Consumer Affairs Department. Suggestions received by Consumer Affairs are initially kept on file in that department. By signing this agreement you will allow us to consider and share your suggestion with others in the company, including Product Marketing and Research & Development. This Agreement is intended to avoid misunderstandings. Please read and consider the terms of this Agreement carefully before deciding whether or not to sign it. Ben & Jerry's will not review or consider a suggestion from you unless you have agreed to the terms and conditions of this Agreement. Please note, if you're under the age of eighteen (18), you must have your parent or guardian sign this agreement.

Most of the ideas which are new and useful to us come from people who work at Ben & Jerry's. Many outside suggestions are already known or available to us, are in our files for future use or development, or have already been tried or exhausted. However, if your idea is strikingly new, unusual or different, we'd like to share it with our Marketing and R&D folks.

By signing this form you will allow us to put your suggestion into our ever growing Random Genius Ideas Database. This database is reviewed from time to time by Ben & Jerry's staff. If we decide to use your idea, we may, but are not obligated to, provide you with a prize or nominal award for your suggestion, such as public recognition, free ice cream or other stuff. Any prize or award for an idea used by Ben & Jerry's shall be given solely at Ben & Jerry's discretion.

In addition to the other terms and conditions of this Policy and Agreement, by signing this form, you represent and agree as follows:

- Any suggestion you send to us shall be owned by Ben & Jerry's.
- The suggestion you sent to us is not confidential and Ben & Jerry's has no duty or obligation to hold it in confidence.
- You are not aware that the suggestion you sent to us is owned or claimed to be owned by a third party or that it infringes the patent, copyright, trademark or other intellectual property rights of another.
- You are not an employee of Ben & Jerry's. Employees of Ben & Jerry's are not eligible to submit suggestions pursuant to this Agreement and Policy.
- Although Ben & Jerry's may, from time to time, provide a prize or award for useful suggestions, it does so in its sole discretion and is not required to do so.
- Any award or prize given to you by Ben & Jerry's is accepted by you in full consideration of your suggestion.
- You do not rely, in submitting your suggestion, on any expectation, understanding, prior communication, or contract you believe is implied, and you understand that only the terms written in this Agreement apply to your submission of your suggestion.
- You are at least eighteen (18) years of age, if not, your parent or guardian has signed the form.

We encourage you to seek any legal protection of your suggestion that may be available (such as patent, copyright, trademark or other intellectual property protection) before you submit your suggestion to us, or to anyone else. We urge you to consult with an attorney if you are unsure of whether, or how, your suggestion may be protected by law, and before submitting any suggestion for which compensation is sought or for which you seek to submit on terms or conditions other than those stated in this Agreement.
This Agreement is entered into in the State of Vermont. It, and any dispute arising under or in connection with it, shall be interpreted under the laws of the State of Vermont (not including conflicts of laws provisions), and, regardless of where you live, you agree to submit to the exclusive jurisdiction of the state and federal courts of the

September 21, 2001

Ben & Jerry's Homemade Holdings, Inc.
30 Community Drive
South Burlington, VT 05403-6828

Dear Consumer Affairs Representative:

You can imagine my surprise and excitement this afternoon when I returned home from my nightly ritual of pilates, to find a letter in my mailbox from you and Ben & Jerry!

Although it had only been a little less than a month since I sent you my idea for a wonderful new flavor I call "JEW CREW", I had begun to have a few sleepless nights here and there, often waking up from dreams in which Ben or Jerry told me my ideas were useless and belonged in the garbage disposal! Can you believe they'd say that? I mean, I know it was a dream, but still.

Nonetheless, all my fears and horrible thoughts dissipated today when I got your letter, accompanied by a wonderful coupon for a free pint of ice cream! I went out right away and bought a pint of Chunky Monkey and ate the entire thing on my couch as I called various family members to tell them of the exciting news that Ben & Jerry were seriously considering my new flavor! I have to say, my Grandma Gertrude was extremely excited about what was going on, and even said "My Goodness" in Yiddish.

Anyway, I've signed your agreement allowing you to seriously consider my wonderful new flavor "JEW CREW" and I will now sit here and wait for Ben and/or Jerry to contact me. Or you, too. I mean, you may not hold the same weight as the co-owners of the company, but I can tell by your demeanor that you're quite a sweet person!

L'Chaim, to life!

David Paulson

264 South Doheny Drive, #8 Beverly Hills, CA 90211

BEN & JERRY'S AGREEMENT AND
POLICY CONCERNING SUGGESTIONS

Accepted and agreed to:

Signed: _David Paulson_   Date: _9/21/01_

Your Name: _David Paulson_

Parent/Guardian's Signature: _____   Date: _____
(if you're under 18)

Parent/Guardian's Name: _____

Suggestion ID: _86976-N_

Please sign this page and return it to Ben & Jerry's using the enclosed postage-paid envelope. Please make a copy of this page and the agreement to keep along with the attached copy of the letter you sent us for your records.

If we decide to use your idea, you'll be hearing from us! If you have any questions, please contact Ben & Jerry's Consumer Affairs Department at (802) 846-1500 between 9:00 and 5:00 EST Monday through Friday.

Thank you!!

December 10, 2001

Ben & Jerry's Homemade Holdings, Inc.
30 Community Drive
South Burlington, VT 05403-6828

Dear Consumer Affairs Representative:

With Chanukah approaching, you can imagine the depression that's been setting in and around me. It's been over three months since I first read the sweetest words from you, singing the praises of my proposed new ice cream flavor "JEW CREW"... And now nothing. Nil. Nada.

I signed your release form. I responded back in a timely manner. I've even purchased a pint of your ice cream at least once a week to keep my mind and stomach in the "Ben & Jerry's Zone", so that when you finally contacted me to tell me that the "big wigs" wanted to make my flavor, I'd be more than ready for the call. But as I've mentioned in the first paragraph, up in the third line – it's been <u>over</u> <u>three</u> <u>months</u>.

My psychologist, who I started seeing back in October, told me that the best way to work through this situation was to express my feelings to you and ask for some kind of explanation so that I could move on. That's what I'm doing here today. (Mind you, I hope you don't think that just because I'm seeing a psychologist that I'm some kind of crazy-person, I just prefer telling personal stories to strangers than my mother since she's so overbearing and quite honestly the epitome of a Jewish mother who just can't deal with the fact that I chose a career that didn't involve filling cavities and ripping out wisdom teeth with sharp metal objects.)

I think if you were able to tell me where in the process my "JEW CREW" is currently sitting, I'd greatly appreciate it. Is it in the conceptual phase? Is it being tasted by everyday people on the street to determine if it's a wise flavor to market? Have your marketing people started to draw up designs for the container? If so, I have a few drawings I'd like to forward that involve sunsets, tropical locales, and sand. <u>White</u> <u>sand</u>.

I look forward to your response! And FYI – Dr. Aames (my psychologist) told me to tell you not to feel as though you're assisting a self-destructive personality, but instead you're <u>encouraging</u> a selfless humanitarian to not become self-destructive. Honestly, it didn't make much sense to me, but then again, I'm not you.

Oy vey!

David Paulson

---

264 South Doheny Drive, #8 Beverly Hills, CA 90211

January 8, 2002

David Paulson
264 South Doheny Dr.
#8
Beverly Hills, CA 90211

Dear David:

Thank you very much for contacting us. It was nice to hear from you.

We're sorry to hear that you are seeing a psychologist because you haven't heard from us about your flavor suggestion. We have the flavors for 2002 already set and ready to go. Any flavor suggestions we received during 2001, will be looked at for possible inclusion into our line-up for 2003. Therefore, if your flavor should happen to be chosen, you wouldn't hear from us until sometime this summer or fall. We make no guarantees that any consumer's suggestion will be accepted. If yours should be, you would be contacted sometime later this year.

In the meantime, to help you through this obviously traumatic time in your life, we've enclosed a survival kit. Please enjoy!

Sincerely,

Ben & Jerry's

Enc.

30 Community Drive • South Burlington, Vermont • 05403-6828 • Tel: 802/846-1500 • www.benjerry.com

September 10, 2001

ConAgra Foods, Inc.
One ConAgra Drive
Omaha, NE 68102-5001
Attn: BUTTERBALL Consumer Affairs

Dear Sir or Madam:

I hope you're as excited as I am. I was recently called and told that I have been selected to be one of six contestants on an upcoming episode of the NBC reality series, Fear Factor! The only drawback, however, is that my episode is set to shoot on Friday, November 23rd, the day right after Thanksgiving!

With that in mind, I must tell you that all my friends swear by the BUTTERBALL brand, and will most likely be feeding me your turkey the night before I'm going to be careening head first off some kind of structure, hundreds of feet in the sky. I have been also informed that it's possible I may be challenged to jump from one moving truck to another as they travel fifty miles an hour side-by-side.

As all turkey contains a drug they call tryptophan, which I'm told causes drowsiness, I'm wondering if I should cancel my appearance on the show in an attempt to escape death and dismemberment. Then again, if I'm okay to do death-defying stunts the day after consuming a BUTTERBALL, please respond ASAP. Thanksgiving is rapidly upon us.

Happy Thanksgiving, early!

David Paulson

264 South Doheny Drive, #8 Beverly Hills, CA 90211

ConAgra Foods Consumer Affairs

2001 Butterfield Road, Downers Grove, IL 60515
Phone (630) 512-1834 Fax (630) 512-1124

October 4, 2001

Mr. David Paulson
264 S. Doheny Dr # 8
Beverly Hills, CA 90211

Dear Mr. Paulson:

Thank you for contacting us regarding Butterball Frozen Turkey. Congratulations on being chosen to appear on the Fear Factor Show.

We have enclosed information on tryptophan that is found in many foods. We hope that you find this helpful.

We are delighted to hear from our valued customers and take pride in providing only the highest quality products for you and your family to enjoy. If we can help you in any way, please feel free to contact us.

Yours truly,

Butterball Consumer Affairs

Record No.: 0084897A   AC

ENCLO 1
SURE

Tryptophan is an amino acid and is found in turkey. It has been shown to help induce sleepiness. Milk contains relatively high levels of tryptophan. Thus, that is why milk is prescribed to induce sleep and deal with light cases of insomnia

In cooked turkey, tryptophan makes up just slightly over 1% of the total protein. The literature shows that 20 to 50 mg of tryptophan per kilogram of body weight per day has no observable affect on an average sized adult. By looking at this as a very conservative measure, a 160 pound adult would need to eat more than 21 ounces of turkey in one day to reach the 50 mg per kilogram per day of tryptophan ingestion

Drowsiness may be attributable more to eating heavy, carbohydrate-rich foods along with turkey rather than to turkey alone

Recent studies suggest that ratio of carbohydrate to protein in a meal influences the synthesis of brain neurotransmitters which are involved in sleep, mood and depression

Sleep is believed to be regulated by serotonin, a neurotransmitter in the brain which is synthesized by the amino acid tryptophan. Carbohydrate-rich meals increase level of tryptophan in the brain and subsequent serotonin synthesis. The resulting drowsiness is caused by composition of entire meal, often rich in carbohydrates at holiday time, when turkey is commonly consumed

Since many people eat an unusually large meal at holiday time, they often associate drowsiness they feel afterwards with turkey. To be more accurate, they should associate their sleepy feelings to the increased amount of carbohydrates consumed, along with turkey

October 7, 2001

Consumer Affairs Dept.
BUTTERBALL
c/o ConAgra Foods, Inc.
One ConAgra Drive
Omaha, NE 68102-5001

Dear Sir or Madam:

Thank you so much for your kind note, dated October 4, 2001.

I've taken the time to read the information you sent me on tryptophan, and I must say that I think I went a little overboard in worrying about this drug! As long as I avoid milk, and keep my turkey consumption to under 21 ounces on Thanksgiving, I think I'll be wide awake for any of the nail-biting stunts I'm going to be challenged to do on <u>Fear Factor</u>!

I had one last favor to ask, Ray. As Butterball has been so supportive in my getting onto <u>Fear Factor</u>, I wondered if it may be possible for you to send me a Butterball T-Shirt? That way, I can wear it on the TV show, and support you in the way you've supported me! I'll promise to not hurt myself, or dirty the logo while I'm participating.

What do you think?

Living on the edge,

David Paulson

September 27, 2001

Mr. Frederick W. Smith
Chairman, President, & CEO
Federal Express Corporation
3610 Hacks Cross
Building A
Memphis, TN 38132

Dear Mr. Smith:

First of all, I must say that I'm quite impressed with the variety of jobs you current hold. Chairman, President, and Chief Executive Officer! I bet you can hardly find the time to watch <u>Friends</u> and eat TV Dinners!! (I do...that's why I mention that. And, on a totally unrelated note, is it me or has Matthew Perry gained like twenty pounds lately?)

The reason I'm writing, however, is in regard to a set of packages I plan on sending through your company to my Aunt Beatrice and Uncle Howie in Paris, France. They've been a loving set of family members for years, excluding the years 1993-94, when they believed that someone in a black car was out to get them, and weren't too cheery when you'd call them on the phone. Nonetheless, I'm planning on sending them a family heirloom, that if lost in the Atlantic, could never be replaced (even if I paid for insurance).

As you may or may not remember, a Fed Ex cargo plane crashed into the water in last year's film <u>Cast Away</u>. And of course, I know it's a movie, but the main character opened some of the packages, and kept some sealed – eventually returning them to their rightful owners at the end of the film. I simply had to ask – if such a scenario really happened, and my family heirloom ended up on an island in the middle of nowhere, would your employees open my package and use them to stay alive? Or would they treat them with the respect that I'm sure you'd like them to treat them with, and return them to my Aunt and Uncle upon being rescued and returned to the mainland?

You may think it's an unreal scenario, or something you'd rather not address, but it's a valid concern when contemplating sending a valuable family heirloom across choppy Atlantic waters, in a plane owned by you.

Kindest regards,

David Paulson

P.S. – I've already contacted UPS on this scenario, and they seem to think that their employees would NOT open the package, and would be sure to return them to the rightful owner upon their rescue. Their only caveat was if the package included food that may be able to save their life (like coconuts, dried fruit, or See's Candies), then in that scenario it may have to be consumed. And you know what, I buy that explanation.

264 South Doheny Drive, #8 Beverly Hills, CA 90211

David J. Bronczek
President and Chief Executive Officer

Delivery Code 1841
3875 Airways Boulevard
Module H
Memphis, TN 38116

US Mail PO Box 727
Memphis, TN 38194-1841

Telephone 901.369.3600

Express

October 25, 2001

Mr. David Paulson
264 South Doheny Dr., #8
Beverly Hills, CA 90211

Dear Mr. Paulson:

Thank you for your letter bringing Mr. Smith's attention to your reflections on what real
FedEx employees would do if they found themselves in a situation such as the one Tom
Hanks' character faced in *Cast Away*.

Most of us at FedEx were very proud of the character's actions and devotion to duty as
expressed in that film, and felt it reflected positively on our best traditions. As you
suggest, the chance of a similar scenario occurring in real life is quite remote, but, as we
all know, especially since September 11, anything is possible and nothing is more
important that the lives saved in a critical situation.

FedEx is committed to a *People • Service • Profit* philosophy. We make money by
providing the best service in the industry while showing the highest level of respect and
loyalty to the people involved, that means to our employees as well as the customers. So,
in the simplest terms, I think we would want any employee in that situation to do
everything they possibly could to preserve their life until they could make it home safely
to the arms of their family. And if they brought customers' packages back with them, all
the better.

We value the trust our customers place in us to handle their priority package needs. I
hope this answer gives you all the confidence in us you need.

Sincerely,

Oran Quintrell
Executive Management Assistant

oq

December 11, 2001

Mr. Frederick W. Smith
Chairman, President, & CEO
Federal Express Corporation
3610 Hacks Cross
Building A
Memphis, TN 38132

Dear Mr. Smith:

I don't know what kind of clap-trap ship you're running over there in Memphis, but I thought I should bring it to your attention that there's some intern named Oran Quintrell running around your offices, answering mail on your behalf. In fact, the only reason I became aware that this individual was an intern pretending to speak for you, is that he gave himself a title that is laughably made-up…"Executive Management Assistant"! Can you believe it? Seriously, it made me laugh for hours.

Nonetheless, as I'm sure Mr. Quintrell stole the letter and shredded it before you had a chance to read it, I will re-state my reason for writing. After watching the movie *Cast Away* starring Tom Hanks, I became concerned about sending a valuable family heirloom overseas via Federal Express.

I posed the question, "What if the plane carrying said family heirloom crashes into the water, and one of your staff members washes up on a desert island with said family heirloom? Would they open it up, thus ruining said family heirloom?"

As I mentioned before, if the item was a fruitcake or some kind of edible item, I would be okay with your staff using it to survive. But opening up my FedEx box simply to parade other people's personal items on a sandy-white beach (mostly due to boredom), is not something I care to take part in.

Simply put, I need to know what the official Federal Express line is on stranded package delivery men. Are they told to <u>not</u> open packages, or are they allowed to? And then, if they do, are they responsible for taking care of them?

I look forward to <u>your</u> response, Mr. Smith. Let me know what college this intern goes to, also, and I'll make a call on your behalf and tell the faculty there just what Mr. Quintrell happens to be up to.

EXPRESS-ing myself,

David Paulson

---

264 South Doheny Drive, #8 Beverly Hills, CA 90211

Delivery Code 4634
3875 Airways Boulevard, Module H
Memphis, TN 38116

US Mail PO Box 727
Memphis, TN 38194-4634

Telephone 901.369.3600

December 26, 2001

Mr. David Paulson
264 South Doheny Dr., #8
Beverly Hills, CA 90211

Dear Mr. Paulson:

Mr. Smith has received your second letter, and has, again, asked me to respond.

I regret that you found my initial response to the hypothetical situation you proposed from the fictionalized account in the movie *Cast Away* to be unsatisfactory in any way. Packages are moved in real time in the real world, and we must, in the end, let our actual record of excellence speak for itself.

I wish you success in making arrangements for the transport of your family heirloom, as well as a safe and satisfying holiday season.

Sincerely,

Oran Quintrell
Executive Management Assistant

oq

December 28, 2001

Mr. Oran Quintrell
Executive Management Assistant
Federal Express Corporation
3610 Hacks Cross
Building A
Memphis, TN 38132

Dear Mr. Quintrell:

Let me first apologize to you for any miscommunication we may have had over the last few months. My original hypothesis, that you were simply a lowly intern answering Mr. Smith's letters as a prank, was unfounded and obviously untrue.

I hope you can accept my apology as I currently have very few family members who talk to me, also the result of such behavior. Like my Uncle Bill, who I had arrested one evening because I thought I saw him rummaging through my car's glove compartment. Years later it was admitted to me that, in fact, it wasn't Uncle Bill at all, but a local transient who people simply referred to as, "The Finger". Needless to say, when Uncle Bill returned to society, he vowed to never speak to me again.

I can finally admit to you, however, that I have fully accepted the fact that Federal Express does have my family heirloom's safety in mind and I must say that your actual record of excellence does speak for itself. After I finish this letter I plan on going down to the local Federal Express hub where I will pack and ship the "Paulson Family Snackster", a wonderful little hot-sandwich maker that my Aunt and Uncle in Europe have been desperate to try out. Quite honestly, you stick a few slices of bread in there, along with tuna and some cheese, and watch out! Instant Tuna Melt! Really, technology has just about gone right over my head.

Thank you again for your patience, Mr. Quintrell. You are indeed one of many useful cogs in the Federal Express machine.

In real time and in the real world,

David Paulson

P.S. – As an avid fan of family lineages, I wondered where your family originated from. With a name like Quintrell I'm figuring it's either Switzerland or Hungary. Well, which one is it?

---

264 South Doheny Drive, #8 Beverly Hills, CA 90211

October 4, 2001

President
Kinko's, Inc. Corporate Office
PO Box 8000
Ventura, CA 93002-8000

Dear Sir or Madam:

While putting together a presentation packet for the local chapter of **The Official Lorne Michaels Fan Club**, (of which I am the President, Treasurer, and Communications Liaison), it came to my attention that KINKO'S seemed to be lacking a competitive edge in one particular area. That area... Contests & Sweepstakes.

What do you say? How about giving your customers the opportunity to win a lifetime supply of color copies? Or a Sweepstakes that will garner one lucky winner their own personal industrial-sized copy machine? Or how about a contest challenging your consumers to write an essay on, "Why Professional Binding Is The Hottest Thing In Today's Society"?

As an observer in the most basic sense of the word, I observe my surroundings and the activities of big-business. And in doing so, the above idea had come to the forefront of my mind. Contests, Mr. President of Kinko's, Inc. Sweepstakes!! It's the one thing standing between your company, and financial freedom.

You may just be a winner, like,

David Paulson

264 South Doheny Drive, #8 Beverly Hills, CA 90211

Three Galleria Tower
13155 Noel Road
Suite 1600
Dallas, TX 75240

October 9, 2001

Mr. David Paulson
264 South Doheny Drive, #8
Beverly Hills, California 90211

Dear Mr. Paulson:

This is in response to your October letter you sent to our president regarding "Contests & Sweepstakes." I wanted to let you know that your letter is being sent to our vice president of marketing for review. If there is an interest in pursuing this matter further, a member of our marketing staff will contact you.

Thank you for your interest in Kinko's.

Sincerely yours,

Kinko's, Inc.

More than 1,100 Kinko's locations worldwide. For the location nearest you, call 1-800-2-KINKOS or visit our web site at www.kinkos.com

⊕ 100% post-consumer recycled.

196

December 10, 2001

Vice President of Marketing
Kinko's, Inc. Corporate Office
PO Box 8000
Ventura, CA 93002-8000

Dear Sir or Madam:

Per your later dated October 9th, I am writing you this letter in regards to Kinko's sad state of affairs when it comes to "Contests & Sweepstakes".

Let's face it, Kinko's is faltering. All around you, companies are giving away luxurious trips to exotic locales, free services, those bobbly-head mascot thingies that people put on their car's dashboards – they're everywhere. And there you sit, in your cushy corner office, making your assistant schedule meetings and pick up your cleaning, all the while ignoring what the public has thirsted for over all these years.

I can sum it up in about seven words... <u>People</u> <u>want</u> <u>to</u> <u>win</u> <u>a</u> <u>color</u> <u>copier</u>. Simple enough, relatively cheap in the larger scale of things, and an amazing opportunity to bring Kinko's to the forefront of every happy copier's mind.

Let me tell you this... On a recent trip to your Beverly Hills Kinko's location, I overhead a woman say to her friend, "Man, if I only had my own color copier, I wouldn't have to come here and pay an arm and a leg for this stuff!" At your Westwood flagship location, a pair of what appeared to be "life-mates" argued over the fact that if they only had a color copier at home, they wouldn't be shelling out thousands of dollars to Kinko's each year.

In a nutshell, the proof is in the pudding. And in this case, the pudding just happens to be a color copier. I'd be curious to know your thoughts on this as I'd be happy to spearhead any local campaign if you need to get started before the Holidays are upon us!

Kindest regards,

David Paulson

264 South Doheny Drive, #8 Beverly Hills, CA 90211

October 7, 2001

Manager/Owner
Raging Waters Group Inc.
111 Raging Waters Dr.
San Dimas, Ca. 91773

Dear Sir or Madam:

Ever since the movie, <u>Bill & Ted's Excellent Adventure</u>, I have been intrigued by your water park. Simply watching historical figures such as Napoleon ride through your water tunnels, happily giggling uncontrollably, put a great big smile on my face.

Years later, here I sit, preparing to bring my little cousin Ari and his friends to your park for his eleventh birthday! But, unfortunately, before I can do so – there are a few safety issues I must resolve.

First of all, I have seen pictures of your water park and noticed that not all of your water slides are completely enclosed. Some, are open on the top, which makes me wonder if it's possible that a small child may accidentally swish over the edge and fall hundreds of feet to the ground.

Secondly, I'm concerned about the amount of water rushing through those tubes. Is it possible that someone could swallow so much of it that they may become bloated, or even worse, choke?

And finally, I'm sure you know the old adage "Don't eat before you swim, or you risk getting a stomach cramp"? As your park serves food, I wondered if you require your park attendees to wait a certain time before getting back in the water? If not, it may be a smart rule to implement.

I'd appreciate the answers to these questions so I may move forward with the birthday party for little Ari. I know he's going to so love it, as long as he doesn't fall hundreds of feet to the ground below.

Swoosh!

David Paulson

264 South Doheny Drive, #8 Beverly Hills, CA 90211

198

San Dimas, CA

October 11, 2001

David Paulson
264 South Doheny Drive #8
Beverly Hills, CA 90211

Dear Mr. Paulson,

We are glad that you have chosen Raging Waters for your cousin's birthday party destination.

Let me address your questions on safety:
1. All of our attractions are designed and built under strict manufacture guidelines, which must adhere to guest safety. Every attraction has height requirements and rider instructions that are mandated at our park.
2. The water flow of all attractions is also the ride manufacture's guidelines to safely run the attraction.
3. We do not require our park guests to wait a period of time after eating food before returning to the water, we leave that up to our guests to decide.

I hope I have answered your questions, and feel free to contact me if you need any assistance.

Sincerely,

Dave Simon
Director of Operations
(909) 802-2243

111 Raging Waters Drive • San Dimas, California 91773-9008
Phone: (909) 802-2200 • FAX: (909) 802-2219 • Website: www.ragingwaters.net

199

September 27, 2001

Kimberly-Clark Corporation
Dept. KLFT-65
P.O. Box 2020
Neenah, WI 54957-2020
Attn: Customer Service

Dear Sir or Madam:

Let's be honest, here. When normal everyday people run out of toilet paper, most likely the only thing left to use in the bathroom ends up being your product – tissues. Mind you, some people end up using napkins and credit-card receipts, but more often than not – it's tissues.

As an avid nose blower, I buy your product whenever I run out, but I have come to a realization that I believe your company should be made aware of. Your tissue products do not work well as a toilet-paper substitute.

As I know I'm only human, I realize I could possibly be using your tissues in the wrong way, thus causing them to not work effectively as a toilet-paper substitute. That is why I'm writing, in the hopes you may be able to shed some light on the subject.

All out of paper-goods,

David Paulson

264 South Doheny Drive, #8 Beverly Hills, CA 90211

**Kimberly-Clark**

October 10, 2001

Mr. David Paulson
#8
264 S. Doheny Drive
Beverly Hills, CA 90211

Dear Mr. Paulson:

Thank you for contacting us about the performance of KLEENEX® Lotion facial tissue in sanitary drainage systems.

KLEENEX facial tissue contains a wet strength additive. For that reason, the tissue does not break down as rapidly as bathroom tissue, and the chances of clogging might be greater. This risk is increased if the sewer system is inadequate or if there are any protrusions in the pipes. To be completely safe, wet strength tissue should not be flushed down a sanitary system but should be disposed of with the trash. For your information, we believe just about every brand of facial tissue on the market today contains wet strength.

We hope that this information responds to your concerns about the flushability of KLEENEX Lotion tissue.

Sincerely,

Betty Hammond

Betty Hammond
Consumer Specialist

BJH/LJS

5887579A

Kimberly-Clark Corporation

P.O. Box 2020   Neenah, Wisconsin 54957-2020
(800) 544-1847

September 27, 2001

Diesel
770 Lexington Avenue
9th Floor
New York, NY 10021
Attn: Customer Service

Dear Sir or Madam:

I'm curious about how your company came up with the name, "Diesel"?

Personally, if I was going to open my own clothing business, the last thing I'd do is name it after a fuel that is pretty much obsolete in today's day and age. It just opens the door to those critics and fashion experts like Mr. Blackwell to say, "Well, your clothing looks obsolete, so it's good you picked a name for your company that communicates just that!" If it hasn't happened already, just wait. Here it comes!

As a child who was beaten over and over again on the school playground simply because of a middle name that rhymed with "GROSS", you can imagine the kind of psychological harm that comes out of a situation like that. So, if it isn't too late, you may want to think about a name change. Something a little less dark and dirty. The word "kaleidoscope" immediately comes to mind. That one's on me, if you're interested.

Kindest regards,

David Paulson

P.S. – I've also noticed that you overcharge for your clothing items as well. I mean, c'mon -- $99 dollars for a belt!?! I say, just get an old piece of rope and tie it around your waist. And that's FREE!

264 South Doheny Drive, #8 Beverly Hills, CA 90211

October 18, 2001

DIESEL USA, INC.
662 NORTH ROBERTSON BLVD.
WEST HOLLYWOOD, CA. 90069
TEL: 310-652-2322
FAX: 310-652-2795
WWW.DIESEL.COM

David Paulson
264 S. Doheny Dr.
Beverly Hills , CA. 90211

Dear Mr. Paulson,

As a privately held company since 1978 with a global volume in excess of $400 million, we've always enjoyed receiving letters from individuals offering an alternative point of view.

While we appreciate the name change suggestion, it would be difficult to do at this stage since we trade in 86 countries worldwide.

Thank you for your interest in our company.

Kindest regards,

Brian Awitan
West Coast Sales Manger
Diesel, USA.

FOR SUCCESSFUL LIVING

September 17, 2001

CamelBak Products, Inc.
1310 Redwood Way, Ste. 200
Petaluma, CA 94954
Attn: Customer Service Dept.

Dear Sir or Madam:

I was recently given a CamelBak Hydrobak for my 30th Birthday from my good friend Jude. As I was just getting into hiking, the backpack-water canteen was a welcome addition to my newfound athletic prowess.

Here's the big question, however. Why does all of the water I drink out of my CamelBak taste like rotten rubber?

Sometimes, mind you, it tastes like stale rubber, but most of the time it's got a rotten/two-week old rubbery taste to it. Instead of a refreshing break on a mountainside, my body's reaction is primarily that of a "gagging" motion, which quite honestly isn't too pleasing.

Is there anything you can tell me that may help?

H2-Oh No!

David Paulson

CamelBak Products, Inc.
1310 Redwood Way
Ste. 200
Petaluma, CA 94954
Tel: 800-767-8725 • 707-792-9700
Fax: 707-665-9231

David Paulson
364 South Doheny Drive # 8
Beverly Hills, CA 90211

September 19, 2001

David,

Sorry to learn of your unpleasant experiences with your new CamelBak. The taste you are getting is from the tubing, not the reservoir itself. I have a couple of tricks for you to try to alleviate that nasty taste.

Step I- Try soaking the interior of your reservoir in a sugar/water solution. Use ½ cup sugar to a full reservoir of water. Make sure to release the bite valve & get this solution into the tubing. Let this soak overnight. In the morning, let all the solution drain out via the hose & bite valve. Rinse very well with warm water and take a taste test. If you still notice any rubbery/plastic taste, proceed to Step II.

Step II- Use a limejuice & water soak. Use 3-5 tablespoons of concentrated limejuice to a full reservoir of water. Again, make sure this gets into the tubing, and let soak over night. Let the soak drain thru tubing, rinse well with warm water & have a taste test.

If both these methods fail, please give me a call at 800 767 8725 x 234 to discuss further options.

Regards,

Consumer Service Representative

September 22, 2001

CamelBak Products, Inc.
1310 Redwood Way, Ste. 200
Petaluma, CA 94954
Attn: Consumer Service Representative

Dear Sir or Madam:

You are a kind person. Taking time out of your busy day to respond to me personally with a step by step problem solving plan for removing the vulgar and noxious taste I'm getting through my CamelBak Hydrobak.

I want you to know that I've already tried step one, which required me to soak the interior of my reservoir in a sugar/water solution. After rinsing it quite well, water still continued to taste like it was coming from an underground sewage plant.

Now that I'm ready to get into stage two, which involves using limejuice and water, I had to ask you an important question. Does it matter which brand of limejuice I use? I vowed a long time ago to never purchase limejuice that comes in the small lime shaped plastic container, as my Uncle Edward was once in a fender bender with a truck transporting a ton of the things, and you can imagine the frustration when we realized that the truck in question didn't have any insurance! Needless to say, our family was made to promise never to purchase said plastic lime containers.

Is there another brand you can recommend? What's your favorite kind of limejuice? Does it matter if you use limejuice that has since expired? A lot of questions, I know, but this is a big thing I'm getting into here – stage two of the process. If I screw this up, and my water continues to taste and smell like an oil refinery, well, there goes my hiking trip.

C-LIME'n up a mountain,

David Paulson

264 South Doheny Drive, #8 Beverly Hills, CA 90211

CamelBak Products, Inc.
1310 Redwood Way
Ste. 200
Petaluma, CA 94954
Tel: 800-767-8725 • 707-792-9700
Fax: 707-665-9231

David Paulson
264 South Doheny Dr #8
Beverly Hills, CA 90211

September 24, 2001

David,

Sorry about your Uncle Edward's unfortunate limejuice related traffic accident. Those little plastic lime shaped bottles were exactly what I was imagining as I gave you the instructions for Step II. Allowing for your reasoning not to want to use that particular brand of limejuice, here are some alternatives.

Fresh limes, use store bought limes & a reamer to extract the limejuice. Limes are often very firm & somewhat difficult to extract the juice from. I recommend that you roll the lime on a flat surface under the palm of your hand firmly back & forth a few times before attempting to extract the juice.

With out making a reconnaissance trip to a market, I believe that there is also a brand called Rose's Limejuice. If you can find this, it too would be acceptable.

I would recommend staying away from anything expired. Although you will rinse your reservoir after treatment, you don't want any expired limejuice residue in there to spoil your hiking trip. If the limejuice scenario fails you, please let me know. We can do an RMA exchange for a new reservoir thru CamelBak. I can't say for sure if a new reservoir wouldn't have the oil refinery taste, but it would be worth a try.

Best regards,

Consumer Service Representative

September 28, 2001

CamelBak Products, Inc.
1310 Redwood Way, Ste. 200
Petaluma, CA 94954
Attn: Consumer Service Representative

Dear Sir or Madam:

I have to admit, you're a lifesaver. After a quick trip to my local TARGET, (where I purchased a gaggle of real-life limes and a reamer), and an evening of rolling limes on my kitchen floor, I was ready to get to Step 2! And twenty-four hours later, there I stood in my bathrobe and slippers, sipping an absolutely refreshing bit of water, no thanks to you and your wonderful assistance!!

First off, I would love to write a letter to your superior so that I may compliment you for all your hard work and dedication in this matter! It's rare that you come across people such as you, who take the time and consideration to help consumers with theiir stinky-water issues.

Secondly, I wonder if I may trouble you for a headshot or picture of yourself? As I'm currently putting together a book I am going to call, "These Are The Helpful Consumer Relations People In Your Neighborhood", I'm getting the pictures of people like you, to grace the pages of this upcoming coffee table book. Just imagine, your face, along with such people as Marjorie Evans (Coca Cola), Bill Grayne (Rogaine), and little Aimee Jo Wilkins (Ex-Lax)! You'll be famous! Maybe not as famous as that awful Richard Hatch from <u>Survivor</u>, but famous nonetheless.

If you could sign it, too, that'd be wonderful.

Camel-Bak on track,

David Paulson

---

264 South Doheny Drive, #8 Beverly Hills, CA 90211

CamelBak Products, Inc.
1310 Redwood Way
Ste. 200
Petaluma, CA 94954
Tel: 800-767-8725 • 707-792-9700
Fax: 707-665-9231

David Paulson   October 4, 2001
264 South Doheny Dr #8
Beverly Hills, CA 90211

David,

I'm pleased to know that my suggestion worked out for you. Enjoy your CamelBak in good health. As we say here, Hydrate or Die!

As for your request, it isn't possible for me to send you a photo of any sort. Our company doesn't publish photos of it's employees even in our own publications. Participation in outside publication is not allowed.

Best of luck to you with your venture.

Consumer Service Representative

ACKNOWLEDGMENTS

Special thanks to the two quirky kids who passed along a set of genes that made me stronger, smarter, more agile, and well, a bit—strange . . . Mom and Dad. If it wasn't for your support, enthusiasm, confidence, and hard earned cash, I may have ended up living some silly existence where all I did was earn hundreds of thousands of dollars each year in a well-respected business environment. Whew! I sure dodged that one.

Thanks to my darling sister, Sari—who's been a best friend of mine at least since we left the house and went away to college. Maybe now that this book is published, she'll finally finish reading the last half.

A big *Six Degrees of Separation* shout out to Gwen Macsai, who had the faith to refer me to her agent Arielle through my wife's best friend's girlfriend's sister's second cousin twice removed. Seriously, it wasn't that many people separated, but you get the point.

Thanks to Arielle Eckstut, my wonderful book agent from the Levine/Greenberg Literary Agency, who saw the potential hilarity in this project and went the extra mile to make it happen. Working with a writer can be trying, especially one who likes to ask *a lot* of questions, and she handled it with a smile and a sense of humor. I look forward to creating more business for her in the near future. Thanks also to my book editor, Becky Cole at Broadway Books. She was a fan of this project from the beginning and thankfully "got" everything contained herein. Her enthusiasm and dedication were greatly appreciated.

Thanks to Chris Emerson, who has the rare qualities of being genuine, funny, and dedicated, all the while working in a place they call

Hollywood. I appreciate his constant energy and enthusiasm when it comes to my writing career.

Thanks to Jeff Schectman (Mr. Glass Half-Empty), Jude Weng, the T.N.S.G. (Fabian Marquez, Jim Mendes, Oliver Oertel, Brad Wiss, and Jimmy Rhoades), Brian Rousso, Chris Barnes, Donna Booth, Sherry Boyd, Linda Brown, Casey Burg, Shirlee Clark, Barry Dinsmore, Donald Durkee, Peter Espinosa, Gary Fitzpatrick, Chris Gorley, Marla Goins Hipsher, Julie Igo, Ira James, Lisa Levi, Amy Maanum, Maritizio Marchiori, Frank Murphy, Clara Norred, Carol O'Neil, Charles Schaeffer, Jenya Stumacher, and Jim Valentino.

And finally, an ultra-special, twelve-gun salute, birthday-party everyday thanks to my lovely wife, Jen. She's been a gigantic fan, a supportive friend, a quirky partner, and a great big help throughout this entire process!

ABOUT THE AUTHOR

Courtesy of the author

When not writing important letters, PAUL DAVIDSON writes for various film and television companies. His past projects have appeared on ABC, USA Networks, VH1, and Dreamworks Television. He lives in Los Angeles.